(

———

A MEMOIR OF WANDERLUST AND ANXIETY

SARA MOSS

Edited by Claire Bidwell Smith

Proofread by Jane Aylen

Cover design by Alissa Dinallo

First edition

This AU English paperback edition first published in 2018

ISBN: 978-0-6482605-2-3

For Cherie and Grant — Mum and Dad.
For DWB.
With love.

"I did not wish to take a cabin passage, but rather to go before the mast and on the deck of the world, for there I could best see the moonlight amid the mountains. I do not wish to go below now."

— Henry David Thoreau

CONTENTS

PROLOGUE

"Oh my *god*, that's *disgusting!*" I was suddenly hot-footed in my gumboots, trying to spit and wipe my tongue at the same time. My little brother, about six years old, was delighted by my horror.

"I wasn't *trying* to hit you," Adam laughed, "I can't believe the poo went in your mouth!"

He'd thwacked a stick into the biggest pile of fresh cow manure he'd ever found while we were playing 'explorers' down in the bush. It was a level up from his usual antics of poking spiders' holes and feigning snake sightings to scare me.

"I'm gonna get you...!"

"You'll have to catch me first!" Adam yelled over his shoulder as he dropped the stick and shot uphill — through the bracken fern, skirting the dam. He was quick when he had a head start; my extra almost-five years didn't always count. Under the electric fence. Almost home.

We played together in the yawn of Australia's summers, and through wet winters in those eucalypt hills. Six hours from Sydney on the old roads, on the mid-north coast of New South

Wales, near Kendall. The incredulous ask of the kids in town, "What do you *do* out there all day?"

"Whatever we want." *After our chores are done.*

By 15, I mostly wanted to play alone.

There were two ever-present giants: the mountain that obscured the reception for our two television stations, and the sensation for which I only found the simplest of words. *Life is waiting. Out there.*

The best dreaming time on the farm was at the top of 'the hill' at dusk. Valleys and paddocks dimmed in magenta last light, kookaburras chorusing in the trees. Sometimes I'd wander and wonder about footlights and chorus lines, and acting school and Broadway. Casually, quietly. Then I'd sing something from *Phantom of the Opera* or *Joseph and the Amazing Technicolour Dreamcoat.*

Another evening at the top of the hill: *I can't believe that relief science teacher asked us today what we wanted to be when we grew up. None of his bloody business!* I'd made some facetious quip about making my mark "via world domination".

Mum always knew I'd leave. She knew I was made for elsewhere. Dad said I had to have a goal.

They came to Canberra when I was 20, to celebrate my graduation with a journalism degree. Before the ceremony, in their hotel room, I carefully unwrapped something heavier than expected for its size. A beautiful small silver ingot; its fine engraving: 'Sara — with love and congratulations, Mum & Dad, December 1998'. I didn't know what to say but I treasured it. Later, Dad captured my studiousness and irreverence when he took a serious and a silly 'cap and gown' photo of me. In the latter, slim tanned legs below my white skirt, brown hair falling just below my shoulders, eyebrows raised and a well-fancy-that grin. The next day, my room on campus all packed — friends wished well and hugged tight before scattering once more — we drove home for the Christmas holidays.

Cicadas roared through the heat haze as I stood in the same place I had for so many years, and looked down to the house, the stock yards, the sheds. The mountain didn't seem so big anymore.

How do we know what we want if we don't know who we can be?

How do we know who we can be, without the world?

PART I

BADLANDS | 2005

AGE: 27

1

Queensland, Australia

Luggage in hand, I folded myself into Dad's hug hello at Brisbane Airport. I was very grateful for it — but it was the wrong man's embrace.

Do I look as haggard as I feel?

It didn't matter. Dad took my bulky black suitcase with the red HEAVY tag on it. He didn't even try to joke to cheer me up. That was a first. We'd be in Cleveland in 30 minutes, where Mum was making everything as welcoming as she could at home.

The early evening air was warm and syrupy as we crossed the car park at the international terminal, aeroplanes roaring on the other side of the building.

"I'm so sorry it didn't work out, honey," Dad said.

"Thanks but it's not really over," I replied as we neared the car.

"Oh? But..."

"I'll talk to him in the coming weeks — we're just taking a bit more time out."

Dad wore his skeptical-worried look.

"Can you smell that?" I asked, as he hauled my suitcase into the back of the four-wheel drive.

"Smell what?"

We were beyond the immediate tang of aviation fuel.

"Blossoms!"

"It's autumn."

"Oh, it smells *so* good."

Is it a mix of jasmine and frangipani? Or just a blend of a million flowers?

My stiff limbs melted into the honeyed air after 24 hours' flying and the stark bite of a long Normandy winter. Then I remembered: you can miss the smell of a place and not even know it, until it curls inside you again.

———

In the first month back at my parents' place, I often made a little cocoon in bed. Sheet and embroidered quilt all tucked around me like a chrysalis. I could fold the quilt back at the top and duck my head under the sheet so the sunlight in my bedroom made a little golden halo.

Sometimes I'd pretend I was in a snug little igloo. I'd just survived a snowstorm but it was still too dangerous to venture out.

I was spinning hope — little golden filaments of it — in my igloo-cocoon. My husband's voice on the phone, just before I'd left London Heathrow: "Just go and see your mum for a while."

I didn't want to get up. Mostly, I didn't want to wake up. Not in a death-wish way, it was just that the world had become a fragile, papery thing.

Or perhaps that was me...

Can't I just be a butterfly already?

When I tried life on autopilot, it hollowed me out further. I was so unused to action without emotion, the disconnection made me feel inhuman. But of course, that was an illusion. The emotion filled me, I'd just never known it before: grief.

I sent flares into cyberspace: emails to friends who were now half a world away when I thought they'd be close for a long time.

How are you? What's going on? Where are you working at the moment and whatever happened with...?

Their replies were little beacons.

———

I walked Cleveland's familiar streets, in the original part of town. Big house blocks, retirees' immaculate lawns flanked by wild, trimmed and potted gardens. I tried not to feel overwhelmed while foreign in my own skin, like I had to practise life again.

Practise.

The word made me think of the piano and my slender, impatient fingers stumbling on scales in my teens. I'd wanted, so badly, to just sit and play. I learned just enough to 'go rogue' — two hands pealing between major and minor keys without sheet music, making whatever bubbled from inside. I got deep enough some days to catch a glimpse of something beyond me. But I never knew what it was, nor did I practise; those scraps of music were not repeatable.

Unlike me and Cleveland: we seemed to be on a loop.

Breathe. Why is it so hard to do this? To just go outside for a walk?

Step after step, black bitumen solid under the soles of my joggers. My clothing loose, my hands empty, hair tied back. No make-up. No headphones. I rarely had keys because Mum or Dad were usually home. I catalogued the differences between my current world and the streets I'd walked in England and France.

This street is very wide; there are no cobblestones.

The gardens here are tropical.

It's autumn but I'm warm.

The sky is huge; the blue is intense. It's very bright.

There are lots of different styles of architecture here, not like the Norman villages.

I can smell the ocean.

I see a ribbon of sea and there is North Stradbroke Island.

———

There had been two guests at my wedding in England: Naomi and Charlotte. Naomi had double duty because she was witness and photographer. We were kindreds and opposites in almost every way but she had also made a tear-streaked journey home from London to Brisbane about a year earlier.

She picked me up from Mum and Dad's in her little red hatchback, with her pink-red spiky hair, and sometimes we'd drive north to Brisbane city, sometimes south to the Gold Coast. She introduced me to her smart and funny new friends.

When it was just the two of us again, she didn't mind when I cried quietly in the passenger seat on the motorway. When I said, "This isn't how things are supposed to be," she'd reply with an arm squeeze and "Oh, honey."

One day she told me everything would be okay in a couple of...years. She'd flinched in place of the well-intentioned platitude and wielded a more likely truth instead.

———

Mum drank gallons of coffee and I drank gallons of tea and we talked daily in the autumn sun on the front veranda. She manoeuvred her chair downwind or stood a few metres away when she lit a cigarette, to avoid me swatting the smoke away.

She'd stood near the end of the same veranda when I had left for London, nearly three years earlier. Mum had said with a smile, "Just get married if you find the right person; don't worry about inviting us, if you don't want to. Weddings are about the bride and groom — do what makes *you* happy."

The precious thing was, she had meant it. I'd waved for as long as I could see her; she'd mirrored my grin.

I'd had a backpack, my camera gear and a little red bag with orange lining. That little red bag had become a talisman in the conversations between me and Mum over the years. It began as a joke, I'd been so besotted with its myriad pockets and zips when I bought it. It was a TARDIS bag. Somehow it became an object of power.

Now, Cleveland. Again. *Again.*

"Don't forget," Mum reminded me mid-hug, whispering close, "you still have a red bag with orange lining — you can do anything."

I want to believe you. I want to feel that.

2

I secretly thought I was part plant. Always leaning towards the sun — *needing* the sun — to photosynthesise happiness. My previous 12 months: autumn, winter, autumn, winter.

University. Maybe I could go back? If I don't go back to France...

I requested course guides for mid-year intakes at campuses in Brisbane and the Gold Coast. Undergraduate programs and master's degrees in multimedia, IT, graphic design, and creative industries.

Scholarships — anyone do scholarships for non-school leavers?

The fees had increased considerably in the seven years since I'd graduated.

I also began requesting submission guidelines from magazines and newspapers that published travel articles. I had to make something of what I'd been doing, damn it. A residual thrill glimmered from my first byline in a glossy magazine — words and pictures — published less than a year earlier about the cottage renovation in Normandy.

When the editor of *Australian Traveller* magazine responded to my query and commissioned a piece on Gold Coast accommodation, it was the only thing that kept my head together.

———

I traded a handful of texts and calls with my husband during several months in Cleveland.

When I spoke to him — on the phone mounted on the wall between the fridge and the pantry in Mum and Dad's kitchen — I ran my fingers along the thin louvres of the pantry door. Smiling, I'd look at the fleck in the cork floor as I asked what time it was there, already knowing the answer.

It was like coming back to the world; his voice the conduit for colour and warmth. For those minutes there was no time and my filaments of hope burned bright.

I borrowed books from the library too. Little epiphanies blazed at my late-to-the-party reading of *Men are from Mars, Women are from Venus*.

It wasn't all bad — my god, we just made classic mistakes!

Untangling threads of my pain, I emailed my husband in an attempt to reveal what I thought had gone wrong and how we could make it work. Hitting 'Send' quelled the vast scooped out feeling that had made its home in the pit of my stomach. It solidified the ground that had threatened to engulf me.

For a few hours, I re-coloured my own world.

———

There are only a few things I remember clearly about when I found out. I was sitting at the wooden outdoor table in the covered courtyard and there were newspaper sections strewn across one end, mostly real estate. I think I'd been noting the accumulation for several days, maybe a week. I'd assumed Mum and Dad were looking for an investment property.

"What's with all the real estate sections, Ma?"

She said something like, "I knew you'd twig," or, "I knew you'd be wondering about that."

My parents were looking for two properties. I had no idea how their budget would stretch that far. Especially considering the four years' sweat, tears and cash they'd just poured into the exacting renovation of their home. That thought was fleeting; the alternative flicked my brain. Or maybe Mum told me.

Most of that memory is smudged into my own opaque despair. But I knew this: my parents were separating after 29 years of marriage, and 32 years after their blind-date meeting in Canberra at the army's Officers' Mess.

I thought: *It's about time. I don't know how you lasted this long.*

I said: "But you've only just finished the reno!"

Everything seemed civil and almost mathematical at that point.

———

Adam lived a few streets from our parents then. He drove his girlfriend and me to pick up pizza one evening a few days or weeks later.

"Back in a minute. Behave, you two," he said in his headmaster impersonation, just before crossing the rainy car park.

When he came back he was crying. About Mum and Dad.

I leaned forward in the back seat and put my hand on his shoulder as he blew his nose and sniffled and failed to stifle another bout of tears. I felt bad for him; I'd rarely seen him cry since we were kids. I'd rarely seen him, actually. He'd gone to boarding school as I went to uni; he finished school as I went overseas.

I really don't see what the problem is. Surely you've noticed Mum and Dad don't work as a couple?

———

Those fraught months in Cleveland had become like stagnant water and my lungs were beginning to fill with it.

I'd taken one last breath and left my husband a voicemail. Something like: "Hi. Listen, I'm just going to get on a plane and come back to London. We have to talk. I want to see you. I want to make this work — we need to do this face to face. I miss you. Call me when you get this and we'll sort out the details."

A text message pinged on my phone a few hours later while I was chatting to Mum out the back. I went into the shed for privacy to read it.

Dad's shed paid homage to ordered accumulation and invention. Leaning against the work bench, I opened the text message from the other side of the world:

 I know I shouldn't do this via text message but I'm just about to get on the ferry and don't have time to make a call from the pay phone, sorry. Don't come back. It's over, Sara. x

I clutched at the bench, kicked in the chest. That's where I unravelled. Near the shadow board for the tools, amid drawers and shelves for neatly gathered garden and building supplies.

Then the toxic little voice from my own underworld snarled: *But why are you so sad? **You're** the one who actually left.*

PART II

TO SEA | 2001–2002

AGE: 23–24

3

Brisbane. I came to you the first time with all I had, car brimming. After university, I'd zoomed north from the farm — on the Pacific Highway for a couple of days. I arrived in your wilting January sun. It made hot shadows near your riparian heart.

River, river, where are you going?

If I'd truly known you on a map first — if I'd let the cartographers speak instead of beelining to my *idea* of you — there'd have been no pang that first weekend when I drove to your coast and I met only mangroves and slips of sand. The beaches, I learned, flaunted further north and south of your river tongue.

Your strangers and strangeness made my new world.

I uncovered you — in that humid swill — one suburb and conversation and photograph at a time. My eyes learning your light. Fellow photography students' faces framed with fresh-cut matting. Architecture; landscape; still life in your humming gardens. *Click.* I took so many pieces of you.

Mum and Dad came to visit in that first year. They left and sold the farm. Once their dream; always my childhood — trees and animals and a cornucopia of books. They came back; to Cleveland, 35 minutes' drive from the city. Nana and Pop came too.

I'd left home twice and once it followed.

Just as you were then, Brisbane, so you would always be: the keeper of things I never expected to find.

———

One February day in Cleveland I turned 23. It was 2001.

Days later, Adam asked, "Where are the flowers for your hair?" as I wheeled my luggage to the courtyard at Mum and Dad's, ready to put my suitcase in the back of the car. My 'little' brother was somehow already 18, taller than me and happy school was over.

"What?" I replied.

"You know," he paused then sang a line from the 1960s hit, "If you are go-ing to San-Fran-cisco..."

I laughed as I spoke the next line, "...be sure to wear some flowers in your hair... Yes, very good."

The classified ad had appeared in the back of *The Courier Mail* a couple of months earlier, just as I was finishing my diploma: 'Wanted — Cruise Ship Photographers'. A stranger had booked my plane ticket and I had a nine-hour layover in San Francisco, on my way to Florida.

Mum didn't like goodbyes but she was brilliant at smiling, waving and holding it together until she was out of my sight. Adam kept humming his San Francisco chorus line. Dad was stoic.

I was finally *really* on my way.

———

She was pristine and all cool-white gleam, cutting a long shadow across the frenetic Florida dock. I craned my neck to look at her top deck. Her insignia-emblazoned dome and lettering on the bow confirmed she was the right vessel. My lips parted in slow-breath awe. I drank in the string of orange life boats, row on row of portholes and glass balconies. Her stern was perpendicular; unlike any ship I'd ever imagined.

It's so big it blocks out the sun.

Raw and ragged, I'd travelled for more than a day from Brisbane. A few dozen of us from around the world were directed off the crew bus and up the gangway in Fort Lauderdale. Accents from TV washed around me — *I'm really in America!* — as I was thrust into the chaos of turnaround day. Each cruise was a seven-day loop from Florida: to the Eastern Caribbean, then, later in the season, an Eastern and Western Caribbean itinerary alternated.

I tucked a map of the ship into my pocket and was directed to slot in with a small bleary-eyed group striding behind a clipboard-wielding officer. We were on the major thoroughfare below decks, the starkly-lit linoleum-floored 'M1'. It ran most of the length of deck four and smelled like dirty steel, old food and disinfectant.

"Crew areas extend throughout all 17 decks, and 290 metres — or 951 feet — from bow to stern," the officer said. "If you hear the emergency alarm at any time of the day or night, always act accordingly and assume your emergency duties unless expressly informed it is a drill," he added.

As a group, we pressed ourselves against one wall to make way for perspiring men who leaned hard into trollies stacked high with suitcases. Others wheeled racks of clothes, assortments of boxes. Several people in jeans and T-shirts — presumably off-duty crew — carried grocery bags.

We detoured upstairs through the world of plush carpet,

timber panelling and brass railings, to see the lifeboats
suspended above the wide timber promenade on deck seven,
then found our way via a different route back into the spare,
utilitarian crew areas, *strictly* off-limits (the officer was very clear
about that) to all passengers.

A siren sounded somewhere out on deck, above the
clattering corridor. *Is that the emergency alarm?*

I just wanted to sit down for a while in a quiet dark room
and eat something familiar. My nauseated layover in San
Francisco had mostly been spent nibbling, when I could, on a
plain bagel. In my Miami hotel room, I'd scratched through a
late-night room service menu and ordered a fruit platter; my
nervous stomach feeling every mile that had pushed me further
from home. So much for a long-anticipated, glamorous foray
into the world.

The officer with the clipboard spun to face us.

Is he about to tell us this is an emergency?

"Don't use the passenger elevators, always use the stairs.
Wear your uniform and name tag at all times in passenger areas.
You'll be informed about the watertight doors, fire procedures
and your muster station, during the safety orientation. Any
further questions?"

I was allocated a cabin with another new starter. "I'll take the
top bunk," she said. I didn't want a fuss so I put my bags on the
bottom bed in the minutes before we had to race off to the safety
introduction, work area orientation and whatever came next.

At 5pm I was officially a photographer because that's when
my first shift in the photo gallery began and all 2,500 passengers
descended. They assumed I knew what I was doing. *They* had
questions.

"What time is dinner in the main restaurant?"

"How long is the pool open?"

"When will my bags arrive at my room?"

"Can I book a tour here?"

"Well, Sir," I'd never called anyone 'Sir' or 'Ma'am' in my life but that appeared to be the done thing, "this is actually my first time aboard too, let me just check for you…"

"Oh that's so cute; you're from England/Ireland/Canada/New Zealand…"

My cheeks soon hurt from smiling. "No, I'm from Australia."

People grumbled about price while they bought their souvenir embarkation photos. My new teammates (we were all 'photogs', it seemed) had taken those photos at the dock, developed and printed them aboard — all before the passengers found their first drink with an umbrella in it. I concentrated on working the digital till.

A fantasy about sleep began to bloom beyond the barrage of questions, sales and persistent hunger pangs.

How on Earth will I find my way back to my cabin? It all looks the same down there. I wish I could have left breadcrumbs, Hansel and Gretel style.

Then, like a set change in an old theatre, the dock I could see from the window opposite the photo gallery counter suddenly began to move.

No, that's not right. The dock's not moving, it's the ship. We're leaving port!

In that instant, my breath caught and it was like the first mid-air moment after jumping off a diving board.

"You're done, Sara," someone said, interrupting my reverie. Another of the international team of 13 photogs had arrived in the gallery for the next shift. "You made it through day one. Only six months to go. See you later at the bar?"

———

"What do you want to drink?" asked the Canadian photog all the girls fawned over because he looked a lot like Leonardo DiCaprio. It was his round for the team.

"I'll just have a lemonade, thanks—I mean, a Sprite," I said. I'd been caught out by that cultural difference already. In Australia 'lemonade' and 'Sprite' were the same thing.

"No, an actual drink. I'm not buying you that," he said.

"Um, well, I don't really drink; I'm not sure what there is..." I felt stupid.

"Okay, I'll surprise you then," he said.

I felt all eyes on me. Several of the female photogs had been abrupt in our conversations so far and not exactly welcoming. But I'd never met any Russians or South Africans before.

Are they just like that or is it me?

Through an intense weariness I smiled at everyone and drank what the Hollywood lookalike bought me: Cointreau and Sprite became my shortcut to fitting in — if I ignored the instant headaches and the way alcohol turned my makeup-free reddish skin aflame, like bad sunburn.

It didn't help that I also blushed easily when flustered, which was how I spent my first restaurant shoot — known as 'ressie' by the photogs — on my second night aboard.

"Sara, what the hell are you doing down here? You're supposed to be upstairs shooting ressie," the photo manager said, briefly looking up from one of the printing machines in the lab that was already turning out images of smiling diners.

"Sorry, I think there's something wrong with my flash; it's not firing properly," I said over the noise, holding up my manual camera, knowing every exposure had to be precise or there'd be all sorts of trouble printing.

"Get her another flash and sync lead," she barked at one of the seniors in the lab then turned to me again, "sort your camera out *before* you go to the restaurant next time, this shoot is really quick, go, go!"

I ran the six flights back upstairs with my newly assembled rig, realising halfway up that I hadn't grabbed more film but I wasn't going to risk a return to the lab.

I'll just see if I can borrow some from someone else.

When I got back to the restaurant, I didn't know who had been photographed. I approached one table, smiling.

"Good evening every—"

"We've already done that," said a middle-aged man, waving me away with disdain, "we're eating, will you leave us alone!"

Finding another photog, I asked which tables still had to be done.

"We're pretty much finished, where were you?"

I started to explain but never finished my sentence; she just walked away. I needed a drink after that evening. Regardless of the consequences.

In the crew bar — and the Officers' Wardroom, which was a hike to the other end of the ship and up seven decks — the tease of close-proximity testosterone and mutual interest was an elixir. "How did you come to work at sea?" became my favourite late-night question, particularly for the musicians and the men with several stripes on their epaulettes. Our conversations were relaxed and easy.

As I returned to the photogs' corridor early one morning in those first weeks aboard, I side-stepped a few colleagues sitting on the floor talking and one of the women pointed at me and grinned, "You've got that look in your eye — you've been *prowling*!" Charlotte was a no-nonsense transplant from Northern England to Canada who was about my age and friendlier than the others.

I thought I was 'exploring' but I guess that's appropriate.

I laughed and retreated to the perpetual darkness of my shared cabin.

"Night everyone!"

That cabin was a windowless microcosm where I struggled with time. Three steps from the door to the bunk beds. If we didn't turn on the TV to check the view from the bridge cam, the only cues from the outside world were the sounds of the ocean or anchor on the other side of the steel hull.

A hush of waves and the constant motion of night-time sailings sometimes soothed. But the daily metal gnawings on industrial anchor chain reverberated throughout the walls when we docked and departed.

Every time that anchor violently ripped me from sleep: *How will I get through this?*

4

My cabinmate wasn't in so there was no one to ask. I stuck my head around the cabin door as the alarm blared in the hallway and three officers appeared.

"Um, excuse me," I said, squinting into the light, hiding my pyjamas as best I could, "is that the emergency alarm?"

A smile flicked across the face of the shortest — a stocky man.

"Are you new?" he barked.

"Yes."

"Right. There's a fire. What are you going to do?"

"We're on *fire*?"

"No, but say we were," he shouted over the alarm, "what are you going to do? Show me!"

"Well, I'd get my life jacket, check for smoke," I said, opening the door a little wider.

"Come out *here* and show me."

The alarm was merciless. I crawled on the floor as best I could with one hand over my mouth, feigning protection from smoke. Braless under my T-shirt and life jacket, with my red boxer shorts-covered backside in the face of three strange men, I banged on cabin doors nearby, yelling "Fire!"

The men watched me for a minute. Possibly it was less. It felt like a long time on my hands and knees, banging, apologising internally.

"Fire!"

Sorry if you were asleep; I don't want to be doing this either.

"Where's the nearest fire extinguisher?" yelled the stocky man, just as the alarm stopped and the other two busied themselves with papers on a clipboard.

"It's just around the corner there," I pointed as I stood up. My fluorescent orange life jacket strapped across my chest preserved a little dignity.

"Right. That's it," he said. The other two men nodded and disappeared. Then, as though we were at a bar, the stocky man looked me right in the eye, smiled and said, "So, where are you from?"

"Australia. Um, are we done here? I need to go and—"

"Drill's finished," he said, and started to walk away. He added over his shoulder sharply, "Make sure you know where your muster station is!"

I darted back to my cabin.

———

On Saturdays I usually had to get up at dawn and dress like a pirate. Fake pistol, scars drawn on my cheek with eyeliner, hook-hand and all. I took the first tender ashore and my bare feet paced fine Bahaman sand off the island of Eleuthera.

"Here they come..."

The early risers alighted — already dressed in nearly nothing — set to spend the final day of their cruise sunbathing, drinking and carving up the quiet with jet skis. They were met with rows of white sun lounges, thatched umbrellas and open-sided bars. But they rarely expected 'pirates' and one last photo op.

"Arrrrrr! I see you there! Come on over 'ere," I said, scowling and corralling the first of many in front of the camera — a firm grip around their shoulders, pistol drawn. The people who played along were fun, protesting that their swimwear gave them nowhere to hide any gold. Others seemed fed up with photographs or cruising. Or possibly life.

My first Saturday there, I became a Cockney pirate. Taking on an East London accent (that I'd only picked up from TV) must have been my subconscious way of making sense of the costume and the ridiculousness of it all. I don't remember which photog I was partnered with that day but I know we hammed it up like street performers. The early rise had to count for something and we were all in.

The temperature rose early too. Felt hats, woollen jackets and the Bahaman sun were not allies. I was soaked with perspiration by 10am; hoarse by 10.30. And I was jealous of The Waiter.

He wore a tux and tails atop swimming shorts and waded to mid-thigh-level water with an empty bottle of champagne and two plastic flutes stuck to a serving platter. Anyone who thought they could escape a photog by going for a swim was wrong. The Waiter faux-French charmed his way into a picture with everyone in the shallows.

We could smell the barbecue for several of the five hours we were in costume and working in the sun. When I finally sat down with my icy drink and hearty burger, I realised I had to return to the ship, shower and change into uniform, and get to the photo gallery for four hours...in 25 minutes. I was starving. Operation Inhale Food began.

I needed energy on all fronts, particularly as I got to know a few of the other photogs.

————

During one much quieter afternoon in the photo gallery, a handful of female colleagues used their go-to method of exclusion: backs turned, all speaking Afrikaans, with the occasional glance at me. They were only metres away. The school playground had come to sea.

Here we go again.

I straightened cameras, albums and photos that were already straight, feigned nonchalance, hoped a passenger would appear and buy something. No one came. I stared out the window, trying to lose my thoughts in the expanse of ocean, recalling the few times I'd had a chance to walk out on deck — circling on the promenade as we ploughed across the water, great engines rumbling; land and real life so far away. Untethered.

Now I was back in the belly of the beast, being silently eaten.

One of the guys on shift in the gallery that day was South African too. A few minutes after the women resumed speaking English, he motioned to me and then the stock room.

"Do you know what they were saying about you?" he asked when the two of us were out of the others' earshot.

"No! I've no idea and it's been driving me crazy. They do that a lot," I said.

"They're really pissed because you're so happy all the time."

"Seriously? Because I'm happy?"

"Yes."

"There's nothing I can even say to that."

So I just smiled. A lot. Particularly at the end of the day — which was sometimes the middle of the night.

I nodded a 'hello' and grinned at the trio playing on the small low-rise stage in the dimly-lit Wheelhouse Bar. I didn't want to break the groove made by those drums, bass and piano. Not while passengers were still around. I tried to sit in an out-of-the-way corner, relieving my achy feet and pretending I was in a basement jazz bar in New York City just washing the day away.

Ice clinked in my glass, conversation pooled around me and the tang of lemon and orange was sharp in my mouth.

Later, when the official shows were finished and the Wheelhouse was almost empty, a couple of guys from the show band brought a saxophone and trombone and joined in. The five men had all performed their standards for the evening — it was time to *really* play. While the bartender ran his close down routine, the musicians jammed. Improv was king and the king was fearless.

I didn't really know anything about jazz but Dad had a heap of Louis Armstrong records and he'd play them late at night every now and then, after a bit to drink. He'd close his eyes, nod his head; one hand holding his glass and the other all clicking fingers and circling wrist. My teen self would sit nearby, waiting for the sensation he seemed to be feeling when he'd open his eyes again, returning from some far-off place, and ask, "Can you *feel* it?"

Nope.

But at midnight in the Caribbean those jazz nuts made me reel. There were hunch-shouldered riffs up the ivory; the piano would strut atop the quick-thrum but mellowing bass line and the high-wire sax blew everything away. Then the trombone joined the fray and a little ecstasy shimmied down my spine while the drums became the pulse. Everything swelled and roared and calmed again; wire brush on the drums and single-handed piano illuminated the echo of a musical frenzy.

I began to breathe again. Letting my shoulders drop, the final wave of primal thrill pealed through my limbs and I wanted more.

Pour more music into me. Play it again, boys.

Later, amid the high hemlines and the low light of the crew bar, the show band rocked the night. The drunken, pheromone-fuelled pulse of the place went crazy.

The guitarist was on his knees, back arched and head almost touching the floor as he made his strings wail. The drummer's sticks were a blur. The band couldn't get no satisfaction but the crew sure did. We were sweat-ridden dancing fiends from around the world in that one room. I kicked back my head with a devil-grin to the ceiling, my long brown hair as electric as my eyes, as our white ship sailed into the black night.

5

T he islands of St Thomas and St Maarten, you're distinct swatches in the Caribbean but I have married you in my mind. I have melded your territories — US Virgin Islands and French/Dutch West Indies — into a montage of swelling morning heat with hustling throngs of taxi drivers; steel drumming buskers and the ring-ting-ting of beachside casinos. I remember supermarkets with fresh food that quickly spoiled in warm air; white sand beaches and souvenir shops turning tricks: including postcards that gave you a refinement the naked eye didn't see.

But how you wooed with the stunning aqua-marine of your shallows.

Sometimes I had time with you. Sometimes I had time with the crew and you: lunch, beer, cocktails. A silken swim in your waters. Officers out of uniform; dancers in bikinis; photogs taking more photos.

I left you. We all left you. Until the next week. The ship's acoustic undercurrent a seemingly looping chorus, "...Wastin' away again in Margaritaville, looking for my lost shaker of salt..."

———

Florida was an onslaught to the senses when we returned to Fort Lauderdale each Sunday. My brain took a critical few seconds to recalibrate each wrong-side-of-the-road turn when I took the crew shuttle bus from the dock into the city centre. Twinned horror and delight awaited me at my first grocery store run: spray cheese actually existed, but so did chocolate ice cream with peanut butter chunks.

And sometimes Fort Lauderdale delivered joy and trepidation in human form.

I'd been adrift amid the foreign for a couple of months — just long enough to doubt my ear.

"Excuse me," I said, leaning towards a young woman I'd been eavesdropping on at a café popular with crew, "sorry to interrupt, but are you from Australia?" Something about her was comforting.

"Yeah, sounds like you are too?" she asked.

I wanted to hug her.

"I'm from Brisbane. Well not originally, I grew up on the mid-north coast of New South Wales, went to uni in Canberra, then studied photography—Sorry, you don't want my life story. I'm *most recently* from Brisbane. You?"

"So am I! Where do you live?"

Her name was Naomi. Our friendship was immediate. We joked later that opposites attract; that was mostly true. She was joining 'my' ship as a photographer.

Now there'll be two of us!

Then trouble walked up the gangway: a flame-haired new boss named Toni.

———

Toni didn't walk, she strutted. She didn't ask, she demanded. One of the most disturbing things was witnessing her laugh and bat her eyelids at senior officers, who sometimes responded favourably. *Careful, or she'll take you back to her cabin and put you in her cauldron.*

"What does she actually carry in those large yellow envelopes?" It was a mystery pondered by half the photo team when it seemed Toni never put them down. Someone quipped: "If she ditched the envelopes, she might have to pick up a camera."

Toni and I disliked each other instantly.

"Where's Sara?" Toni asked the photogs on shift with me in the photo gallery.

"Oh, she's just gone to the bathroom," one of them said.

Silence. Almost on cue, I reappeared around the corner.

"Where were you, Sara?"

"I just went to the bathroom," I said.

Her eyes narrowed and head slightly cocked. "I don't believe you," she said.

Are we in Grade 1 here?

"Well, whether you believe me or not, that's where I was."

"Keep those breaks to a minimum. You're here to work," she said — before disappearing, yellow envelopes clutched to her chest.

My roster became peppered with back-to-back late finishes and early starts. She'd cut me off or dismiss anything I raised in team meetings. It became a bit of a team in-joke. While she had me in her crosshairs, everyone else was 'safe'. Well, mostly everyone.

The dreams began sometime around then too — powered by memory and my nervous system to make the work day perpetual; a maritime 'symphony' of waves and anchor underscoring them all.

There was the restaurant shoot that didn't end.

Forever cajoling passengers into a photograph while they ate, overcoming their resistance to being quiet for a moment, finishing their mouthfuls; ladies quaffing hair and worrying about fresh lipstick; fat, boisterous men, waving away our 'insolence'. Or the line trotted out so many times in real life, I lost count: "Oh, don't take a picture of me, I'll break the camera."

There was the photo gallery shift that didn't end.

Thousands of images taken each cruise were displayed on wooden panels that swung together and locked shut when the gallery and shop were closed. At sea, they were open 9am–10pm but there were invariably last-minute browsers — "Oh, can I just buy this one before you shut?" For each eleventh-hour purchase, there were also the passengers who didn't actually want to buy anything, they were just galled a staff member closed a panel in front of them. They made their displeasure known. In the dream, the panels to close — and the passengers to politely rebuff or to serve — multiplied endlessly in a kaleidoscopic hall of mirrors.

On the short-sleep mornings I startled to the alarm — *didn't I only set that a few minutes ago?* — ghost-walked into my uniform, dead-weight limbs unrestored by a shower and quick breakfast. All my loving thoughts of bed were discarded at the threshold of the photo lab where I'd pick up the gallery keys and any passenger film that had been printed on the overnight shift, and trudge, with my large water bottle, up the first six flights of stairs for the day.

During the climb to the photo gallery I hankered for the deep sleep of life on land, where there was no back-of-mind worry about an emergency in the night, when the safety drill would become real and the lifeboats had to be launched into distressed darkness.

I promise I'll sleep more tonight. I won't listen to jazz with the

musicians; or go to a crew corridor party; or sneak onto the bridge
with the navigator. Even though the late-night quiet is lovely up there
and when he puts his hand in the small of my back and presses me
against him...

"Hey," Sadie greeted me.

We worked together often because Toni appeared to dislike
Sadie too. She got a bunch of early and late shifts that didn't
seem right for someone who was only one level below assistant
photo manager.

Is Toni threatened by Sadie?

I enjoyed Sadie's stories; she'd gathered quite a few during
more than four years at sea. Because she was engaged to an
Australian, she was one of the few Americans to whom I didn't
have to repeat myself. One evening on a gallery shift I trusted
her with my American accent.

"You sound like you have a brain injury," she said, laughing.

"Oh. Really? People have told me it's quite good," I said.

"Were they from the US?"

"Hmmm. Fair point. Are you on shift in the morning for last-
minute sales too?"

"Of course."

"It always amazes me that people who've had a week to buy
their photos would suddenly want them when their bags are
packed and they're about to leave."

"That's when they think they can get them cheap."

"Oh, that makes sense. And explains why they get so angry
about us 'just throwing them away'... Huh. Let's see how many
people we can shock when they ask how long we have off until
the next cruise."

"What do they think we do? Jet off to our beach house for a
week and come back when we feel like it?"

"Six hours, madam. We have about six hours until the next
cruise..."

"And don't forget 'When's your next day off?'"

"Ah yes, 'In six months, madam. We get on the ship, work for six months and have our next day off at the end of our contract.'"

Sadie did her best impression of a horrified passenger. Coiled into my tired bones was the knowledge the food, beverage and housekeeping staff had it even worse. In several ways. They were aboard 10 months straight, living in the metallic-smelling depths of the ship, and were woken at an uncivilised hour every morning with a metal ladle rapping on their *four*-to-a-cabin door.

———

"Don't get me started on her," said one of my engineer friends as he sipped a beer in the Officers' Wardroom. "Your boss is a nasty piece of work."

"So it's not just me then?" I asked.

"Some blokes like that sort of thing but keep her away from me. The way she treats people..." he said.

"What can we do?" I was getting fed up.

"Well, there's one thing we could do," he said.

"Yeah?"

"We could put a ball bearing in the ceiling of her cabin. Y'know, so when the ship rocks it will drive her nuts and she won't be able to find what's making the noise."

"Brilliant! Would you?"

He looked sheepishly into his beer and we never spoke of it again.

———

Toni increased the team workload by creating new shifts.

"We have to make budget," she snapped in response to a

small, quiet chorus of sighs and sagging shoulders in our team meeting. Her eyes widened further at any questions, which she branded as "disrespect", her voice whittling to a sharp chirp.

Was she a bully at school too?

In a couple of months, Toni had accrued allies among new senior staff who joined: they had worked with her before and *liked* her. My new cabinmate, the assistant photo manager, was in that faction too. However, seven of the photogs agreed life at sea was rather miserable on her watch. And Sadie and I had made a sobering calculation about our own rosters: we were working for less than $5 per hour.

The rebellion began.

I crafted an email to shoreside management. It was brief and polite but straightforward about the lack of professional conduct from the manager. The email noted team morale was low, and that Toni was unapproachable and uncooperative when it came to trying to solve workplace problems. Would they please help?

I encouraged my unhappy colleagues to email management with the same message — and they did. We were quietly confident things would change.

Surely they will do something if they know what it's like out here. We're at sea, not in a labour camp. I'm sure Toni couldn't be this rude and dictatorial if we were in an office on land.

6

W e sailed into the tail end of a hurricane one day and were quickly climbing water mountains under dark skies. The larger the waves, the quieter the ship became: a water-borne, semi-deserted theme park ride. There were few human voices. The groan of the vessel and wet roar and slap of the wind and sea eddied through late afternoon.

I pushed with my quads and calves to get 'uphill' in the usually horizontal hallways, then trod slowly as we plummeted again on the other side of the waves, resisting the urge to run. Rolling side to side wasn't as easy to combat because it was less predictable and varied in its angle of lean. Pitching and rolling together as we sailed towards dinnertime wasn't ideal.

Forever prone to motion sickness, I wondered when the nausea would start.

Charlotte was my partner for the evening, and we ploughed up and down the interior corridors towards our assigned restaurant for a shoot. I gave in to gravity and grinned; I felt fine, even a little excited — like a kid ignoring the 'No running!' sign at the local swimming pool.

Oh, I should be careful not to hit my flash against the walls...This is fantastic!

A few hardy souls were eating in the restaurant.

"No, Sir, you're not looking green at all but I understand."

We only got a handful of photos. Charlotte and I had a chance to talk, intermittently staggering a little before righting ourselves as the ship did the same. We were also allowed to sneak back into the galley and scoff a slice of cake or two.

Full of dessert and oddly content, I dropped into a dreamless sleep on the tempestuous sea that night, wondering if it had taken a hurricane to cure my motion sickness.

But minor miracles were in short supply.

———

Toni sat, sour-faced and silent, while the assistant photo manager chaired our weekly team meeting.

Well, well, what's this then? Has management had a word?

We all had brief individual meetings scheduled with the Staff Captain to discuss the photo department.

Yes! My email must have worked. So much for 'don't get shoreside involved'.

Things were about to change. But not as I'd hoped.

After Toni sulked for a few days she increased gallery shifts from four to *eight* hours after our pirate shoots on Saturdays — when most of us worked a 16-hour day prior due to photo shoots for formal night. Her disdain for me and Sadie appeared as fierce as ever.

A few photogs wished they'd never said anything. I wasn't one of them.

———

What is that?

The sea was calm. We — a few photogs and musicians, lingering at the bow, well after midnight — stared into the water a few storeys below. Our collars and tongues loose; name tags pocketed. I'd just helped pack away the last of the portable but heavy portrait backdrops and lighting after another evening's shoot.

"There! Did you see it?"

Greenish spark lines rippled either side of the bow, flaring briefly underwater, like liquid Northern Lights. The way I imagined the Northern Lights, anyway. A sliver of moon made us little more than silhouettes in warm air. My eyes adjusted and I saw the magic: pockets of flickering water, as though reflecting noon-day sun, all around us.

Phosphorescence.

We were somewhere off Mexico, I think, on one of the Western Caribbean sailings where the time zone was kind and we picked up an additional hour each night for half the cruise. Whichever sea it was — transfixed at the bow in my still-neat uniform, the wash of camaraderie around me in the great, delicious world — I fell in love with everything.

I had ached for that sensation, to be beyond all I knew. To feel the world was a boundless and bountiful place. I was all loose-jangling excitement again, work worries forgotten for the moment. Possibility whirled like some effervescent force inside that could only escape through my grin. Maybe I moved a little closer to the guy leaning on the railing next to me, I'm not sure, but I do know I wanted to live fiercely. Whatever that meant.

We steamed into the night, salt made our skin tacky, our conversation tumbled easily into the waves and the silence beyond. The phosphorescence almost wired itself into my brain then. It was sure, magical footing — while everything was in motion.

The queues had shrunk at the bank of pay phones by the dock and there was time to call home. Mum and Dad were the push of about 28 buttons away, in what was beginning to feel like another galaxy.

"Mum! You're home ... Yes, I'm in Fort Lauderdale, about to get back on, we're leaving soon. I've been shooting embarkation photos today ... Yeah, I'm fine. A group of us — Naomi, Charlotte and the gang — went to Miami the other week, felt like I was in *Miami Vice* ... No, still had early sales with Sadie and gallery in the evening ... Yep, we're sailing the Western itinerary now; the water near Mexico is a-mazing ... Grand Cayman is by far the nicest island. Oh, found out I'd need 10,000 US dollars to start an off-shore bank account there. The concierge/security guy was pretty rude; I could have been a dressed-down millionaire! ... What's happening there? ... Has Adam found a job? ... Is Dad around? ... Okay, yeah, should do I s'pose. Love you ... 'bye!"

Whenever I could, I made my way to the top deck at the beginning of each cruise. The crackling energy of 'sailaway' was contagious and the quayside apartment dwellers of Fort Lauderdale didn't seem to tire of waving back at the departing ships, even flicking their house lights off and on. A tiny reflection of the revelry afloat.

Cruise staff — part of the entertainment division responsible for running deck games and quiz nights, and ensuring general passenger merriment — worked the crowd and encouraged everyone to dance. Leis were dispensed with abandon. Bartenders were swift and smiling while keeping up with the cocktail orders. Under a dusk-lit sky the band rocked the amplifiers until well after the first stars appeared.

One evening a new entertainer arrived and sang with the

band for sailaway. Within minutes he had everyone clapping and he appeared to be genuinely enjoying himself. It may have been his first or his thousandth performance, but as he ripped through a Robbie Williams song I became one of the enthralled and the night closed softly around us.

Well, hello. I shall have to find you later, Music Man.

7

The cruise staff team appeared to glide when they swept past the photo gallery on formal nights. They gracefully plied the decks: the men in tuxedoes, the women dazzling in their own dresses. Ever-smiling listeners and problem solvers.

It was enough to make a frazzled photog in flat shoes pay increasingly close attention.

They never had to process and print negatives overnight or try to photograph everyone as they boarded, disembarked, ate and stood awkwardly in front of studio backdrops. They never had to deal with bug-eyed apoplexy induced in some by the prospect of paying $20 for an 8"x10" portrait produced by professionals.

I don't want to get stuck as a photog. I'd probably be better — and have way more fun — as cruise staff. What's going on behind the scenes for them? Are they as united as they appear? How are their schedules? How long are their contracts? How much do they get paid?

I had a new focus for my below-deck conversations. It helped that I already knew most of the cruise staff and they were happy to talk. So was their boss.

"Who would I get to promo the photo department with me on TV if you transfer to cruise staff?" joked the cruise director — cruise staff manager and head of entertainment aboard.

"I'm sure you'd find someone else," I said.

Hamming it up with him on shipboard TV was some of the best fun I had at work. I was sure Toni had recently assigned me that task because she thought I'd be embarrassed or would make a fool of myself on camera.

"So, tell me more about what you've done in the past that would make you a good fit for this kind of job?" he asked.

"Well, I can talk to anyone," I said, "I've been a tour guide at the Australian Institute of Sport — I did that while I was studying — and handled all sorts of groups there, from the general public to schools from across the country to private tours with visiting dignitaries."

"Where is that?"

"In Canberra. People always think Sydney is the capital but—"

"Yes, I know Sydney is not the capital of Australia," he said, "What else?"

"What else do you know or what else have I done?" I smiled.

"Oh, hello! Look out ladies and gentlemen," he laughed. Then, deadpan: "Just leave the jokes to me, would you?"

"I studied drama at high school and also did a few performances at university, so that and the tour guiding means I'm comfortable with an audience. I haven't used a microphone much but I'm sure that wouldn't be a problem; I learn quickly."

Somehow — I don't remember if he suggested it or I asked — I picked up a cruise staff uniform from the crew office and scored a trial run as an assistant to one of the current staff members at a couple of events.

My excitement vanished when Toni found out. She wouldn't authorise it.

The cruise director may have pointed out she couldn't govern my time off. So I volunteered as an event host in my limited spare time, hoping for a transfer endorsement. I co-hosted bingo and word got out to the upper echelons aboard that I wanted to switch departments.

———

The bass could be heard way down the crew corridor. Streamers on the floor and balloons on the ceiling thickened as I approached. I nodded and dispensed a "Hey!" here and there, to a few familiar faces, some of whom didn't recognise me straight away because I'd actually changed out of my daytime uniform. I needed more than grey pants and a navy-blue polo shirt for this.

"Looking good, Sara!" said one of the production guys. The hubbub of conversation and music was amplified as I opened the door to Music Man's suite-like quarters and found the real party, including a bathtub full of ice and assorted alcohol.

How I miss having a bath!

"You came!" Music Man raised his hands as though he was cheering, when he saw me.

"Yeah, said I would, it's quite the party!" I yelled. I got the nod-and-wink-and-see-you-later look, as he tipped the neck of his beer bottle towards me.

We kept making plans to see each other ashore and work seemed to keep getting in the way.

The only time I'd managed to get him alone was when I took his photo for the shipboard newsletter. I was a hands-on photographer with everyone; I found it simpler to adjust someone's pose than to explain what I wanted them to do. There had been a moment when I'd stepped forward to tilt his shoulders — becoming swiftly aware of the current around his body; imagining water or electricity, all the things that shouldn't mix but I was drawn to; I could see he felt something too, our faces so close, a flicker of a glance to each other's lips — and it would have been so easy for us to kiss. I'd lived a few decades lying next to him in that instant but he hadn't closed all the gaps in time and space between us.

Now a few dancers kept him busy in conversation. I found other people to talk to and slowly circled back around to Music Man's part of the room. I created a few excuses to touch him; he reciprocated and an electric shimmy whipped me. There seemed to be an unspoken agreement we would keep it a secret when we got together.

Good god, I can't stand it much longer.

Seconds later a huge bowl of chocolate was being passed around the circle that had congregated and his lips were suddenly on my skin, eating an M&M out of my belly button, tongue lingering a moment. I gasped and laughed. He did the same to a couple of the other women nearby. I wanted an encore in private; I only had a few weeks left aboard.

———

"I know we've had our differences but I thought you might like the chance to get rid of me," I attempted to joke with Toni when only the two of us were in the lab.

"What are you talking about?" she said.

"You weren't happy with my trial for cruise staff because I'm a member of the photo department, I understand that. That's what I was hired for. But I don't think this is the place for me. So I have an official departmental transfer request form and I'd appreciate it if you'd sign it," I said, holding out the paper.

Toni looked at the form and noted I already had shipboard endorsements from the three highest ranks below captain.

"You want me to recommend you for a transfer to cruise staff?" she asked.

"Yes."

"Leave it with me," she said flatly and returned to what she'd been doing.

———

None of the crew was ever exactly sure when they'd disembark. We were all given a contract end date — presumably for admin and sanity purposes — but it could be shortened or extended with minimal notice, depending on staffing needs. So my departure countdown was a loose but hopeful one.

Back to real food and sleep; no uniforms, safety drills or cabinmate. A different boss.

'Ship time' was its own entity too. Weightier; compressed *and* telescoped. Intense. Six months at sea was like two years ashore.

My final week was strange. The last cruise. An ending mostly welcome but one I couldn't quite grasp.

Who will I see again? Where will I sail next? What will it feel like at home without a different place outside every other day? This will be the last time I...

Naomi, Charlotte and Sadie were with me in Cozumel, Mexico, on my final gangway shoot. The task was always the same: to guide every passenger to pause and have their photograph taken as they left the ship. It took about four hours, we worked in pairs; there was a trick to keeping people jovial as we stood between them and their holiday ashore. Albeit briefly.

When we were finished, in a deliciously wasteful celebratory gesture, we cheered and unspooled blank 35mm film into the stark sunshine, holding onto one end of the film and throwing the canister out like a streamer.

"I never have to do this again!" I said.

The girls continued to cheer.

Let's throw more film!

A few days later, at 2am, I was in the middle of a photo team shot (without the senior ranks, of course) taken in the Officers' Wardroom: three guys and five girls, holding beer bottles and making 'bunny ears' all in a laughing entwined group hug.

At 4am, in disbelief, I tucked my farewell card in the front pocket of my bulging suitcase while I finished packing. My passport was returned to me two hours later and I received US immigration clearance.

That was it.

Music Man would sing to another crowd but he'd stay in my head. We were sure we'd see each other again.

Someone else would shoot 'embies' that afternoon as new passengers boarded; the other photogs would sleep or do a grocery store run or load more supplies from the dock.

Someone would replace me. It all began again as I was high above the Pacific, on my way home.

My last thought before exhaustion whisked me to airborne sleep: *I'll make another transfer request to shoreside management when I get back to Mum and Dad's. Just because Toni didn't recommend me for cruise staff, doesn't mean this is done. When your prospective boss — and some of the most senior people aboard — sings your praises, that's **got** to be enough.*

8

ello again, Cleveland. Mum and I talked late into the night; sometimes Dad joined us. Mum told and re-told her when-I-was-your-age stories: torrid tales of power and debauchery from the frontier-like world of early 1970s Canberra. Cruise ships and their incestuousness, it seemed, had nothing on a few former cops, solicitors and outlaws of Australia's capital.

The world of wild house parties and double dealings I was hearing about from Mum didn't reconcile with the city I'd left only a few years earlier. The Canberra *I* knew was all suits and bureaucracy and ADFA boys (from the Australian Defence Force Academy), with a dash of bohemian flavour from the Arts department at the Australian National University.

We change as much as places do, I guess.

It was several years before I remembered it again: in that quiet winter, when I was regaling my parents with anecdotes from my first ship and fishing in my suitcase for souvenirs, my Dad, at the same age, had been at war in Vietnam.

Unfurling my legs — just out of my parents' driveway, heading towards the water — it felt good and strange to be running. After all those sea days, it was the land that felt unstable. Like I had to adjust to the non-movement; my inner ear ever-ready for the rebalance that wasn't needed. My breath, ragged in an embarrassingly short time, slowed me to a walk. I gulped air. A tight chest and hamstrings reminded me cardio still wasn't my friend. But the tingle in my limbs was the beginning of wanting to feel fit again.

It shouldn't be too hard to get into shape...

There was a small park and a little old fisherman's cottage by the mangroves at the end of the street. I liked that the cottage was all dilapidated timber and out of sync with the modern houses nearby. A low-tide-methane cocktail squirrelled into my nostrils as I stretched my calves, leaning on the back of a freshly-painted timber seat.

At dusk, whole squadrons of mosquitoes would rise along that foreshore. Across the bay was North Stradbroke Island, with its inland lakes and majestic sweep of long beach on the eastern side, facing the Pacific Ocean.

It wasn't a conscious thought but I had the sense the clock was already ticking in the back of my mind

How long until I fly over you again, great ocean?

———

I was asleep at my ex-boyfriend's place when two planes flew into the World Trade Centre in New York. It was about 1am on 12 September, 2001 in Brisbane.

Several hours later I woke to my ex on the phone to his boss, who told him to turn on the TV. We stared at the footage; dumb. We looked at each other and spoke in half-sentences over cups of tea for a while. It emerged a plane had also crashed into the

Pentagon; and another about 112 kilometres (70 miles) from Pittsburgh.

His kitchen had a 1970s etched-cream-lino floor, sheer curtains and windows facing the city skyline, with mustard-yellow stained glass panels at the bottom. The walls were a faint pastel mint colour. When it rained, the earth-scent wafted up through the first-floor flat — the whole city dripping in diamond light when the sunshine re-appeared.

We had experimented in the same kitchen a year earlier: "How much cream should we add to the sun-dried tomato pasta so I don't feel sick — you know, like I did when we splurged on that meal in Civic one night? Look, you can get yellow curry paste and mix it with coconut milk. Let's try that."

Our five years' together mattered. Even though we'd both thought it would only be a summer fling. We'd been to the same high school and got together when I went to university. We survived a move to Brisbane too.

Then I went to sea.

We were trying to be friends.

All television stations were looping the footage of the Twin Towers collapsing.

Everything had changed.

———

When I was growing up, our farm had been on a training flight path for the Royal Australian Air Force. Their fighter jets sparked an ancient thing in my bones. I'd sense the engines ripping apart the atmosphere just before I saw them, generating a great belly-churning thunder. As my hairs invariably stiffened along my arms and a dark thrill struck me, I'd run outside, scanning the sky.

Where are you? Where are you?

Sometimes, if I'd felt them early enough, I'd stare at the silhouetted pair of F/A-18s as they streaked low over the treetops. My eyes locked on; the rest of my world abandoned. The greatest occasional reward: a sonic boom.

After puberty, I thought my reaction to the jets was a kind of lust. Some fleeting primal urge to bathe in power, speed and noise. It wasn't learned or taught; I rarely spoke about it. I didn't know what to do with it.

Is this normal?

After 9/11, I realised fighter jets weren't just for training and flyovers during fireworks displays. Amid my visceral reaction to their roar was an unwilling acknowledgement of their menace. Of their necessary lethal power.

Those jets are hunters.

For a month or so no one knew if there would be a travel industry to return to; the fear was potent on the airwaves and in street-corner conversations. And cruising seemed... frivolous.

Or perhaps it's more necessary than ever?

The calendar kept turning over. And everything kept changing.

———

The cruise director I'd met said my transfer to cruise staff was approved. We were just waiting for the shoreside team to make a ship allocation.

Mum and I went shopping. I needed a second formal dress for the nights I'd 'swan' — as it was referred to by crew — keeping the passengers smiling. I usually hated buying clothes but this was different.

As I ran my hands over the embroidered bodice of a dress, I felt like a princess; I did little half-twirls left and right to hear the rustle of the black sheer over the crimson satin skirt. It bloomed about my ankles as I spun.

I look like a rich Elizabethan woman. Or someone an 18th-century artist would paint: a study in a dim room of the fall of sunlight across pale skin and into the folds of the most elegant dress the sitter owned. Possibly with strands of dark hair falling loose from a bun; the woman staring straight out of the canvas, making the viewer wonder what she'd been thinking as the artist was making the portrait.

The vision fell to pieces as my heels hit the floor again. I'd been standing on tip toe as I looked in the mirror, the accompanying black high heels yet to be purchased. Nothing could remove my grin — even though I was pooled in the dull unflattering light of a change room.

"I'm actually going to get paid to wear this. How cool is that, Mum?!"

"It's *very* cool," she smiled at the change room entryway.

It was going to be perfect. I'd get to travel and perform while making others feel good. People often told me I was an excellent listener too.

Sometimes all people need is to be heard.

No more Toni or gangway shoots or all-night printing!

I can save my cash and buy an apartment.

Please let me get the same ship as Music Man...

———

"What is it?" Mum asked, a week or so later.

"They sent an email — my transfer has actually been denied," I said as I offered her a sheet of paper. I'd printed out the email, as though somehow that would change what it said, or make the message more comprehensible.

"What? But they'd approved it!"

"It seems that must have just been from the ship; it wasn't

officially sanctioned by shoreside..."

"Then why were you told it was?" She was so disappointed for me.

"I don't know. The only option I have — if I want to return at all — is as a photographer," I slumped into a chair; tears stung my eyes and a fire pit of anger simmered around my chest, "and I have to let them know so I can be queued for ship allocation."

"Oh, darling," she hugged me.

No cruise lines were hiring. Everyone was jittery. From the outside, it seemed the whole of the USA was one big security clearance zone. The UK and Europe — where I'd jealously watched uni friends go a few years earlier — seemed almost as fraught. I didn't pretend to understand the mechanisms at play but all the global shifts seemed seismic. For the first time, Australia felt more safe than boring. But I still wanted to travel. *Needed* to travel.

Two months later, I was almost out of money when I got the call. I left my beautiful new formal dress at home.

———

"Hello, Sara," said the photo manager. The voice was just as I remembered it.

"Hello, Toni," I said. "Here we are again, eh?"

Of all the ships and all the managers... You will not see my disappointment.

My first ship had been almost new; the second was not. Everything aboard looked tired after 10 years' sailing. Most of the photogs' cabins were below the waterline, in the stark steel world of the ship's bowels. So I slept in a metal box underwater and tried not to think about it.

But twice daily — around midnight and dawn — came the reminder of our potentially dangerous place of rest: the great wailing siren and orange flashing light that accompanied the opening and closing of the watertight doors. One of the 42 doors that sealed the ship into vertical partitions on decks one, two and three was just around the corner from my cabin. They weren't only impervious to water — they ran on a hydraulic system designed to ensure that, once the door was moving, nothing would stop it.

"Do *not* try a Hollywood-style dash through a closing door. The last guy who did that lost an arm," said the safety officer at induction. "I'm serious. Do *not* do it."

I wonder how many times he's seen people try it on their way 'home' from the crew bar...

Though I hated the shriek of the closing door alarm, I was more afraid of the disaster that could trigger its use.

It'll probably never happen.

I tried not to think about it.

After a few days, Toni summoned me to the photo lab: "I want to talk to you."

Here we go.

"Sure," I said, purposefully upbeat.

While I don't remember our exact exchange, phrases have taken root in my mind:

Her: "I don't want any trouble from you. Not like last time."

Me: "I don't want any trouble either. I'm here to do a job. I'll be happy as long as things are fair."

Her: "We're a team here. I don't want any disruption. Shoreside have promoted you, it's up to you to prove that wasn't a mistake."

She couldn't see me perspiring in the navy-blue polo shirt. She didn't know my heart and stomach briefly merged into one racing, churning super organ; oxygen, adrenaline and defiance raging — sick that my eager-to-please nature stopped me from doing the one thing I really wanted: to punch her in the face.

9

New Zealand, I never dreamed of you. You were 'just over there'. A hop, skip and a jump. Dreams were for Paris and New York and London. You were a backwater at best, I thought. I'd never have chosen you. You were another kink in my plans; a geographic anomaly.

But you revealed yourself slowly in the summer of 2001–2002.

The ship made three days' rough work of the snarling, spitting Tasman Sea crossing to find you — Sydney, Melbourne and Hobart in our wake. Respite and grandeur awaited in a rugged pocket at the southern tip of your South Island. Glass water at Fiordlands, imposing peaks like up-turned dragon's teeth. Gales cut with Antarctic chill held no sway that day; no rain came. You were a shining myth made real; I was the one adrift.

Northwards: Dunedin, Christchurch, Wellington, Tauranga, Bay of Islands. Switchback in Auckland and repeat.

"Why can't I use these coins?"

It was a common question at the photo gallery, usually delivered in an accent from the American South.

"Because we're in New Zealand now. That's Australian currency."

"So?"

"Remember those three sea days we had recently?"

"Yeah?"

"We were sailing between two different countries."

"New Zealand is a different country?"

"Yes."

———

I roamed the decks during the New Year's Eve celebration at sea, photographing couples and friends. At midnight, confetti, streamers, balloons and music filled the ship's atrium. Tuxedoed wait staff were on-hand to refill empty champagne glasses. A crazy English photog was my deck-roaming partner that night. We jumped in front of a motley-red backdrop the portrait photogs had been shooting at for hours, grabbed the 'love boat life ring' with the date in the middle and flashed a grin.

Click.

Our smiling, bow-tied selves in formal uniform — long-sleeved white shirt, silver-black patterned waistcoat, black skirt or trousers — captured for a future album. Maybe in time I'd forget the sensation behind my smile.

I don't feel part of this. I don't know where I'm supposed to be but it's not here.

———

Just as a storm begins as a breath of air across a millpond, it all happened very gradually, the seasickness.

Food would not sit as it should.

I must've eaten something a bit off.

My balance flickered. Occasionally little moments of dizziness swirled.

I'm just tired. I need an early night. No 'prowling' this evening!

Serving passengers in the photo gallery — reading the digital till screen, checking signatures, answering questions and bantering about the awful weather — got harder.

Going to lie down, not an option.

I'm fine. Breathe deeply. This is just temporary. I got through a hurricane before!

"Sara, you look awful, are you okay?" asked one of my teammates not on duty as they happened to walk past the gallery one afternoon. I was looking out at the nasty grey squall we were battling.

"I don't feel good at all."

"Go and sit in the back for a few minutes, I'll mind the gallery," the angel said.

"What if Toni comes past?"

"Don't worry about her, you just go."

What if I feel like this from now on? I can't work at sea if I get seasick. What am I going to do?

Nothing felt right.

———

I busied myself with the machinations of work: I took portraits on the grand staircase (also known as 'the Titanic shot'); processed film; dressed in a koala costume and stood outside the main restaurant — the Antipodean version of the pirate souvenir pic in the Caribbean.

On a few occasions, I found a 'lost' image for a passenger when the common complaint, "I can't find my photo!" rang through the gallery, and it proved to be true. The practice was then to sort through long snakes of negatives hanging on the wall in the lab — looking for one frame amid hundreds — print it and dash back to the gallery or call the passenger when it was ready.

At night, the musicians still played jazz in their corridor.

Andrea Bocelli poured into my headphones while my French cabinmate had her Hungarian lover to stay. When the women were spent, four feet protruded from behind the closed curtains that ran the length of the bunks. As I drifted, I found a married man for a little while, and neither of us was interested in resisting the other. *People think they know me. Not so much the 'good girl', eh?* Our secret was invisible in public and in his room — at any time of night or day — it was all a mad, covert, this-feels-like-I'm-more-alive-now kinda wonderland.

————

At some point I met Nick, a cheeky pianist in the show band. It turned out he was from the same area in New Zealand as my best friend from photography class in Brisbane.

"You're a smart Kiwi, how does it feel to be an oxymoron?" I'd joke. Nick would produce a searing vocal Aussie parody in response and I'd roll my eyes. Many of the crew thought he and I were a couple because we'd often finish each other's sentences, but we weren't — I just felt like I'd always known him but hadn't seen him for a long time. Somehow we were kin. We went ashore together sometimes, or with a few other musicians and photogs.

New Zealand had its way with me. I found the pastured hillsides, protected valleys and mirror-surfaced lakes with old timber jetties. Desolate beaches somehow held my gaze as I shivered on their sand. Settler-built stately homes and gardens lured me with their architecture, history and prestige; a visit to each piquing my long-held wish to see Scotland.

I ate my way along the coasts too. Homemade cake, scones with jam and cream, and buttered slices of thick raisin toast sated my appetite in cosy cafés that still burned braziers to ward off the summer chill.

———

One February day in Auckland I turned 24. It was 2002.

I'd been aboard about two months. The best present: Toni was gone. Her contract finished. The second-best present: Music Man called the photo lab on the off-chance I was there. By a delicious miracle the expensive ship-to-ship call connected while I was on my own.

"Happy birthday, gorgeous!" came the familiar voice.

I had a countdown going until I was to see him again: five months. By then it would be nearly a year since we'd been in the Caribbean, almost-touching.

"Ah! it's really you! I'm so glad you rang…"

We'd finally get together when we could *be* together. We planned to cruise on holiday after our current contracts; to enjoy life as passengers for a little while. He told me what he wanted to do while we were cocooned away in our cabin, with no responsibilities other than to ourselves. My breath caught for a moment when I imagined it. My whole body enjoyed the spike of anticipation.

After an hour my cheek muscles were sore. I hung up the phone and I could fly.

Fuelling the spark, after the call he mailed me a letter and several intimate photographs.

 Send me some back...xx

Isn't someone having a fling with you the perfect person to take a few snaps to send to your would-be other lover? Jealousy won't be a problem...

My envelope sent in reply had a few images I had to print myself while no one was in the lab. I was proud of myself for remembering to crop out my head.

Shared secrets were binding me to Music Man. The bitter-sweet balm of distance turning each articulated longing into a promise.

I had the night off: a celebratory indulgence only made possible by the new photo manager, who'd decreed to the team that no one should work on their birthday. His jovial addition, "She might even get a shag tonight!" was a throwaway line and we all laughed.

The crew bar was a dim, dark-timbered room with forest-green and navy vinyl seating. I went that evening in a sparkly red tank top and rarely-applied lip liner, my wavy hair liberated from its usual ponytail. Everyone wanted to buy me a drink; I told people I wanted a photo with them instead.

It's my 24th birthday — I never get to do this again. I want to look back on these photos and remember having a good time with new friends at sea. Just relax. People do that. I've heard it's fun.

———

Summer became autumn.

We sailed north, along Australia's East Coast. My sea sickness subsided.

Near the Whitsunday Islands — all dreamy postcard vistas mid-way along the Queensland coast — I stood in the sunshine on deck, my face tilted skywards and eyes closed, and took in deep wells of ocean breeze. I stretched, admired the azure sea and dreamed of my own hammock on a white sand-rimmed island nearby.

Soon the wondrous, precious ecology of the Great Barrier Reef was behind us.

Someone on the ship had always been there before. Wherever *there* was. All the secret spots and no-go places ashore had already been found — last week, last season, last year. But there was also always someone on the ship who had *never* been there before. Wherever *there* was. Daring and inquisitive, the uninitiated were easy to spot amid the wearied crew who'd already been everywhere and lost the T-shirt long ago.

A pre-emptive buzz built below decks.

I have no idea what I'm doing but maybe things will be okay. Maybe I just have to ride this out. Whatever 'this' is.

10

A sia. You were worlds strung somewhere between transcendence and squalor. For five weeks, the ship traversed your sprawl: into the mouths of giants; through perilous straits, their lantern-lit fishing boats bobbing in thick-ink night.

My first glimpse of you was early one Tuesday morning in March, off the coast of Malaysia. An industrial-looking horizon emerged from the post-dawn sea smudge. Grey water, pink cloud.

I found your Blue Mosque in Kuala Lumpur — architecture, exultant; two female teammates with me, in purple robes and yellow head scarfs as we lay onto our film the mosque's great domes and arches and latticed walkways. Each frame far too small for the history.

In my high school Japanese class, I'd made hundreds of Hiroshima-bound paper cranes. For the Peace Memorial. Besotted with origami paper, I'd barely been able to bring myself to crease its intricately-patterned softness — as though the study of those squares at the right time and in the right light could reveal a life secret. Japanese had continued to shape my tongue and furrow my brow at university; the lecturers possibly perplexed at my lack of enthusiasm for the skill I had.

But my first time in Japan came to this: I spent more than the price of my first car on camera gear; and found a little red bag with orange lining.

There was only one place I really wanted to go while I was with you, Asia. It was another complex stitching of beauty and bloodshed.

———

Julie was my new cabinmate and like the big sister I never had. We sat on the back deck of the ship and stared at the mangroves. They were the only greenery around and it was more pleasant than looking at the rusting shoreside factories, spewing more pollutant into the already dirty scene.

The river that bore us was wide and brown, and the sky looked like it should have been white but had been wiped with a soiled rag. We'd already admired the tiny-framed Vietnamese women ashore in their fine silk dresses. We commented on the clash between them and the foreigners wearing loud shirts and too little sunscreen, piling down the gangway onto waiting tour buses, set for the haul to Saigon, more than 90 minutes away.

Amid all that, there was a memory from a few years earlier I couldn't shake but didn't share.

Dad had never talked to me about the Vietnam War. Until he agreed to give a speech to other people's children about it, at the local high school as part of the seniors' study of war and peace. He wanted to rehearse what he'd written.

In our lounge room at the farm, while I'd been home on a university break, Dad wanted my opinion. Mum's too. He'd never asked my opinion on anything and I'd never heard him ask for Mum's either. What happened next was like having a front row seat to a movie I'd been forbidden to see.

Dad led us into the jungle's dank heart, rifle in hand. We walked through dripping undergrowth; sweat, grime and stench burrowed into our nostrils. We hadn't been dry for weeks; worms tried to dig into the sodden flesh of our sockless feet. Fungus didn't only bloom on the forest floor. The enemy were ever-present but mostly invisible. They made booby traps. Their stealth, ingenuity and territorial advantage had been underestimated.

A young man, only a few years older than I, was in charge of 30 Australian infantrymen advancing in that part of the jungle. For a breath, I was struck by the burden of others' lives. My eyes welled as I fused a few black and white photos of Vietnam in our albums with this first-hand trek, weighed by weaponry and rations and responsibility. It was a glimpse at the chasm.

That man in charge was rehearsing a speech; reading to his family. All his men came home but I don't think that was mentioned; it was just one of the threadbare facts we knew.

Dad had never looked expectant before, not that I'd seen anyway. After I cleared my throat, Mum and I assured him it was a well-written speech, that he shouldn't worry.

On that semester break, I'd seen the man, not just my father, for the first time.

Now the ship was docked in Phu My and the tour to the Cu Chi Tunnels left early in the morning and returned just before sailaway. I wanted to go. To feel claustrophobic and imagine the rats and traps in that underground network used by the Viet Cong during the war.

It would be my way of bearing witness; honouring.

I had asked to change shifts, explaining why that particular shoreside venture was important to me. But the work schedule didn't change. I was left with the view of the mangroves and the memory of Dad's speech and all the music from *Miss Saigon*. I knew every song. I held tightly to the music in my mind while I appeared nonchalant with Julie.

As we sipped soft drinks on the deck in the sticky heat, our conversation went something like:

"What we need," I said, "is a job that lets us travel."

"And pays *well*," she added.

"But doesn't work you into the ground."

"One where you get to meet interesting people."

"And have time off to explore new places."

I suppose this will have to do for now.

We smiled wryly. I think we returned to our own 'tunnel' below decks. Those negatives weren't going to print themselves.

———

At the dock on the outskirts of Nha Trang, there was a cluster of dirt-floored houses. Electrical cords ran erratically and precariously along the street. They looped from house to house and over window sills, powering domestic hot plates and microwaves. An occasional mangy dog skitted past me as I walked. A few market stalls sold brightly-coloured sarongs and T-shirts, alongside pirated CDs for $1 each. I bought a white T-shirt with two pale blue dragons and 'Vietnam' embroidered on the front.

Showing Julie later, I held the shirt against myself.

"I really like it but I don't think my Dad will. He was in the war. Best not to wear this at home, I think," I said.

"You can't live your life for someone else, Sara," she countered.

———

Shanghai burned into my brain.

On deck for the pre-dawn sailing into the mouth of the Yangtze River, an industrial reek of grease, smoke and petrochemicals lodged in the back of my throat. The thick air felt brown before I could see it. At the docks, I'd smell the fetid sea creatures, dead and exposed by the tide.

From the wide, one-mile strip of pedestrianised riverbank known as The Bund, I looked across the water to admire the gleaming grey and magenta baubles of the Oriental Pearl Radio and TV Tower. The tower looked like a minimalist space ship ready to launch; prepared to surrender its dominance of the skyline for triumph in another world.

The traditional white-walled buildings in Old Town looked golden in early light. They had roofs that curled upwards to ward off evil spirits. Old men dreamed in tea houses; red paper lanterns hung from eaves. I bought a small brown teapot glistening with an odd green-gold-orange fleck. Two handleless cups that could fit in a child's palm made the set. It was unlike anything I'd usually buy. It was ugly. I paid a fortune for it. I didn't care. I was taking a piece of Shanghai with me; the leviathan city, just beginning to wake.

I scooped an apple out of my bag and ate it as I walked.

Closer to New Town, black cables cut the air between buildings flanking narrow urban streets. Festooned above roads and alleyways were undergarments, shirts, trousers and linen. A metropolis had its wardrobe in the air. Somehow the whites were impervious to stain.

I found what I was looking for at the edge of New Town. I pushed the cold metal handle of the grimy glass door and entered a war zone. In that crazy-loud internet café, row-upon-row of serial gamers didn't use headphones as they blasted their digital worlds to pieces.

I logged in to Hotmail and sent a stream of news to Mum

and Dad. Good news. Light but true: haggling in Hong Kong; no
Sling in Singapore but wow, that city's clean! Beach time in
Thailand, *real* Thai green curry; going to Wuxi Gardens
tomorrow... There was a moment while writing that email, amid
the gamers' explosions:

I'm in Shanghai; a few days ago I was in Hong Kong and I'll be in
South Korea next week. Perhaps this is the shape of the life I could
never see when I imagined the future as a kid. **This is** *'out there'.*
What was I actually expecting?

———

Nick knocked on my cabin door, mid-morning. I half-hid behind
the door as I opened it, hair a mess.

"You're not even up yet?!"

"I'm so sorry, I can't come today, I know I said I would but I
really need to sleep," I said.

"Being friends with you is like being in a bad relationship —
and there isn't even any sex to compensate!" he fired,
uncharacteristically angry, and walked away.

I was stunned. But very tired. I got back into bed. I
surrendered to sleep before guilt had a chance to flower.

Weeks later, as Nick and I continued to forgive each other's
foibles, we were at an outdoor café somewhere in Asia and I
confided something to him that I hadn't told anyone else
because it sounded so stupid to say out loud.

"I feel like nothing is happening in my life," I said. "I want
something to happen, you know? I want to fall in love or have a
whirlwind romance. I want to explore the world and maybe
have my heart broken a few times..."

Of course, I had someone in mind for the 'whirlwind
romance' but I didn't talk to Nick about Music Man anymore. I'd
done so once and discovered he didn't like Music Man's 'type' —

words he'd almost spat as he recoiled — and that tangent had been abruptly dismissed.

Nick's usually jovial demeanour changed. His expression tightened briefly into one I hadn't seen before. He then tried to soften his response with a laugh that didn't quite meet his eyes.

"Be careful what you wish for," he said.

———

I accompanied a handsome officer to his cabin one night, after we'd been admiring each other for weeks. He was all contrast: pressed white uniform, slick black hair; rapid-fire Italian, languid English. We were kissing and began to undress on his bed, embracing and unbuttoning all at once.

Before I was completely naked, I realised he was stronger than his light-looking frame suggested.

He kissed my neck and whispered into one ear, "I could kill you and no one would know."

Holy fuck. Don't react.

"I'm not in the habit of visiting cabins without telling anyone where I'm going," I said.

Yes you are. Look like you're not fazed. Get out slowly. He could actually be a psycho.

"You know what?" I said, "I want to do this properly, when we've got *way* more time. I've got a very early shoot — it's already morning — let's continue later tonight, hmmm? I'll meet you back here." I kissed his mouth as I pulled my body away.

I dressed and left. He didn't try to stop me. I didn't tell anyone. We skirted the opposite edges of any rooms we found ourselves in after that.

———

Unease — fast flowing, like an underground river — ran through most of my waking hours. I had what I feared were premonitions about something happening to my family. Watertight door alarms bored into my already-broken sleep. The cat calls and numerous volleys of 'Ciao bella!' from several male crew members below decks weren't faintly amusing anymore. They were predatory.

It's 7am. Piss off. I just want to get some breakfast and start my day.

Then: *Is this how I want to be spending my life?*

The ship became a tunnel with an exit point too far away. The walls were closing in. I still had two months on my contract. Aboard we were gearing up to cross the Pacific to San Francisco and sail north to Alaska.

Everything made me angry. Except the thought of seeing Music Man earlier than planned.

During another stop in Shanghai, I took my mobile phone to the top deck late one morning and made a brief but very expensive phone call to Mum and Dad.

"I can't do this anymore. I'm coming home."

11

Mum and Dad were having a barbecue with friends and the smell of cooking sausages wafted in to the room. I'd stolen away for five minutes to check my email.

One new message. *Music Man!*

He said we couldn't cruise together; I'd ruined our plan by leaving my ship early; something about going to find himself.

What?

His excuses stuck like cold stones halfway down my throat. I re-read the email several times.

I had to re-join the group outside and try to eat and act like nothing had happened. Mum saw through my ruse and squeezed my hand as we all sat down, plates heaving with steaks, sausages, fried onions and salads.

During a written question-reply volley with Music Man during the next 24 hours, I tried to unravel all his contradictions. I couldn't. I wondered into my pillow in the darkness.

*What about all our plans? I believed you... I told you so much... I **showed** you... Oh god, am I the biggest idiot; are you laughing at me now? Did I mean anything to you at all?*

Then the empty, shivery kind of upset descended. I'd been moored for so long to the idea of him in my future in some way. I dragged his corpse with me for days.

What will I do now?

———

It had been a whispered word in the back of my mind for years. It became a siren call. Immutable. It tugged at my imagination and my stomach, whetting my appetite for the *real* world and its flash of possibilities. Not the constraints of cruise ships and their 'it's-Cozumel-it-must-be-Thursday' timetables. It whizzed through my thoughts as I went to sleep and it conjured new sensations in my dreams. I had to go there.

———

Mum and I were out wandering one afternoon — enjoying Cleveland's quiet streets and each other's company.

"You're bored, aren't you? Where are you going next?" Mum asked.

"Is it that obvious?" I laughed.

"Well, it has been three weeks since you got back..." she said with a smile.

"I'm going to move to London." I tingled as I said it.

"Okay. When?"

"In a few weeks."

"Better air out your suitcase again."

"I think I'm going to get a backpack this time. And I reckon I'll stop over in New York."

"What a good idea."

———

"Two," was my answer when friends and acquaintances asked me how many people I knew in London. "My friend Samantha, who I met in Brisbane while we were both photography assistants, and Charlotte, a photographer from my first ship."

"Only two people? You must have a job lined up to go to then?" was the usual response.

"No. I'm just going to see what I see," I'd reply.

Why are some people so scared of just doing what they're drawn to?

———

"Once you do this, it's gone, you can't get it back," Dad said.

"I know," I replied.

"This isn't why your mother and I set it up," he added.

I cashed in an endowment policy my parents had started for me on the day I was born. Dad would decry that for more than a decade afterwards. But while I packed, he still flew to Canberra and back in a day on my behalf, to get me a two-year working holiday visa for the UK.

———

This is it. I can feel it. I can feel I've already gone even though I'm still sitting here — leaning against the wall, on the floor of my room at my parents' place in May 2002, looking at the rosette around the ceiling light and thinking how beautiful this house will be when it's renovated. I'm here, on the floor but in the future too, looking back. To right now. When everything inside me is coiled, waiting, ready. I am ready. This is the division, the decision point. There is everything that's already been and all that happens after this.

PART III

MAP MAKING | 2002–2005

AGE: 24–27

12

Manhattan, you were laid out before me for a few moments as the bus from JFK to New York City swept high around a bend. A conglomerate of steel, concrete, brick and glass pushing skywards. Each building a finger of grit and power, dreaming of the clouds. It was late morning. Below my eye line, your roads were perhaps great shadow-streaked furrows, impervious to sunshine except near noon.

From that very brief vantage point on the elevated curve of motorway, you — fabled city — were almost a 2D cut out. Your great throbbing ravines of life on footpaths and escalators, in elevators and the subway, were invisible but they flared for a moment, iridescent in my mind.

I was filled with all the fragments of all the stories ever attached to that glimpse of your exoskeleton. All the circus and dirt and ambition; everything we can bake into what we build.

Anticipation billowed around my body and the bus window could have fogged with my soft, enchanted "Aaaaaaahhhhh" but it was just before summer and the glass had no temperature as my palm pressed it, pushing towards you. The heart of you. The world I would only drop into for 24 hours.

―――――

By the time I unhoisted my bags from my shoulders at Grand Central Station that day, I had a suspicion backpacking was not for me. My new, tightly-packed rucksack had mostly been in the cargo hold from Brisbane to LAX to JFK. But when I carried it on my fine frame — *and* my camera bag — I felt anchored and slow. The home-on-my-back idea of portability didn't liberate me. It made everything feel effortful. I wanted to glide.

So much for being intrepid! Nothing to be done about it now. Wow, this station lives up to its name.

One of the guys from the show band on my first ship met me in the soaring, frenetic cavern of the train station. We jostled, all smiles amid the clamour, into the street in search of my accommodation. It took a little finding. A nondescript door; cramped stairs; feverish carpet. Musty air and an air conditioner in a sealed window that had likely not been opened in several decades. Everything in the room was a bit stained or partially broken. It was only for one night. It was the closest to Midtown I could afford.

We trekked to Times Square for a late lunch. He enjoyed playing tour guide even though he lived upstate.

Soon I was a compass that couldn't find north.

I swung, below the surface and unknown to my friend, from intense excitement to a shallow, unplaceable fear. The pavement was solid but it didn't always feel that way. My stomach churned. I was nauseated and began to perspire. I had no name for it all.

Perhaps I should say something?
Say what?
We could stop somewhere.

Stop where? And do what?

I kept the broiling sensations in my body to myself.

In a café off Times Square, I made slow inroads with the largest side salad I'd ever seen while refusing ranch or blue cheese or any other type of dressing. As my friend and I swapped stories, I tried to re-anchor myself in the full-bodied delight I'd felt only days earlier at the prospect of my trip — my *move* to the other side of the world.

As I pushed more lettuce onto my fork, I concentrated hard on when I picked up my plane ticket and itinerary. How the airport abbreviations signalling time in New York, London and Rome fired big-screen wild-coloured movies in my mind about Great Days To Come.

The wooziness hadn't gone but I smiled more convincingly.

New York, I am really here. Just for a moment. But I am here.

Aboard my British Airways flight to London the next morning, just as the plane began to cruise in the vast, stark blue and the sun lay upon my lap I felt it: the balm at the base of the stratosphere. I basked.

13

"Do you want anything from the shop?" Charlotte asked. She'd come to meet me at London Heathrow — we were at her place, my bags not long put down. I was working out how to be useful or where to put myself in the sparse basement flat in Acton, West London, that she shared with her boyfriend. They'd only moved in 24 hours earlier.

"I'd love a Snickers, or some sort of chocolate bar like that," I said, fishing in my wallet for change.

I knew her partner a little from my first ship too; a blue-eyed Italian with a ready smile who looked at Charlotte like she was a goddess. Charlotte had confided to me at sea that he wore better shoes than she did. It was high praise.

I offered a gold coin: "Is one pound enough?"

"That's enough for about three chocolate bars," Charlotte said.

It was an expansive in-between moment. Liminal. *Everything* was yet to be discovered.

Twilight came so late. Eventual darkness, around 10pm, found me smiling in my makeshift bed on the floor of the front room. Jazz oozed into my headphones. My mind danced as my limbs softened. The saxophone outlined that edge-of-sleep state and there were no words in my head, just the fullness of a sense of becoming. Becoming what? I didn't know.

London, London, I'm here. I found you...at last.

The next day, the three of us trekked back from Argos on two buses and up a steep hill, with half the newly-purchased contents of a household between us. Crockery, cutlery, a dish drainer, washing rack, ironing board... We ordered some of the chaos in the flat and I drifted in my jet lag — thrilled and weary in the first days of an English summer.

My memory wired together a mosaic of architecture, accents and social artefacts in those first weeks: London Bridge, the River Thames, the National Portrait Gallery. BBC TV and *Time Out* magazine. Sainsbury's supermarkets, semi-detached houses, Cockney rhyming slang. Pounds and pence; black cabs, red buses.

I quickly learned 'Boots' was not a shoe store, it was a pharmacy. 'Orange' was not a colour, it was a phone network. 'Chippy' was not slang for 'carpenter' as it was in Australia, it was slang for a fish and chip shop. I walked and walked and rode the underground — the Tube — and got black gunk in my nostrils, the beginnings of my acquaintance with its acrid subterranean tang.

———

I thought I was doing the decent thing, offering to work the remainder of the week when I'd only been there for three, but the Irishman got very close to my face, with his eyes bulging and white skin rapidly flushing a deeper shade of red than his hair. For an instant I thought he might hit me. He flung his arm toward the doorway and extended a pudgy index finger instead.

"Leave now! Just go!" he shouted at the end of his tirade, droplets of spit landing somewhere behind me.

He was a mad man. I hastily changed out of my photo lab uniform shirt in the back room of the shop then left. I was released into early afternoon on Putney High Street — in a pleasant river-fronting area in south-west London. The radio in the lab had played Sophie Ellis-Bextor's *Murder on the Dancefloor* several times per day. Those sugar-pop lyrics gave my step a little oomph as I wandered, aimless for a while under a clear sky on the busy street.

There was still a good nine hours of summer light into which I could lose myself. But I had a few things to do back at Charlotte's. I hadn't planned to stay there for six weeks.

"Sara, we need you to look for somewhere to live," she'd said. Something like that. Definitive.

"Oh, yes, I have been," I said. *Oh no, I hadn't actually told her that I was seriously looking. Now she thinks I'm just sponging.*

When it became clear the photo lab wasn't going to be a long-term option, or even a short-term one, I looked beyond London, to the one place I thought it most likely I could get work quickly.

Apologising for my overstay, I left a card and a gift on Charlotte's kitchen table and slung all my belongings across my shoulders. Leaving Clapham Junction train station, the myriad tracks looked like snakes shining, sunning themselves. They briefly burned golden as I charged over them to England's South Coast.

———

I trudged alone from the seafront towards Portsmouth town centre, a few kilometres away, seagulls still chattering above in murky evening light. My jacket warded off the first shower. I dug out my umbrella and re-hoisted my bag; the backpack irked my tight shoulders. There were also bags under my eyes after two wearying 84-hour weeks.

My new fellow cross-Channel ferry crewmates had made a beeline to a hostel by the waterfront, prior to a big night of drinking on our first shore leave. All the cries of "See you in a week!" had only just faded as the group disappeared around a corner, while I walked in the opposite direction.

Where am I going? I didn't really think this through... I don't know where to go. I'll just head towards town and work it out, I guess...

A homesick pang boomeranged inside me. *Was Dad right? Was this whole trip a mistake?* At the precise moment that thought had formed and registered, I looked up from my already sodden shoes.

Across the road, emblazoned in large lettering on a wide, squat, dark-brick building was 'Royal Sailors' Home Club'. I had no idea what it was but I thought working on a car and passenger ferry made me a kind of sailor, even if not in the traditional sense. It was a tenuous link but I had nothing to lose.

Maybe they can recommend somewhere for me to stay.

During an awkward conversation with a receptionist — in which I tried to hide my ignorance of the function of the place, while she became increasingly confused — the manager was summoned. A spritely middle-aged man appeared from behind the timber panelling into the warmly-lit, soft-carpeted lobby. He ushered me to one of the banks of leather chairs.

I told him I'd just started work on one of the ferries, making three crossings of the English Channel each 24 hours, and I would be sailing out of Portsmouth. My roster would be two weeks on/one week off. But, regrettably — an unfortunate business — I'd not secured lodgings for my time ashore. Perhaps he might be kind enough to make some enquiries on my behalf regarding a suitable place to stay that would still be within my means? Not that one ever likes to talk about money, of course. But sometimes...

The kindly man seemed perplexed but delighted.

My working in the duty-free shop didn't seem weighty enough to mention, and I certainly didn't say there was a vacuum cleaner dedicated to removing rough-seas vomit from the carpet. So, to cement my seafaring credentials, I launched into tales of hurricanes on the high seas and was sure to mention the gross tonnage and top speed of the two cruise ships I'd crewed because that was the sort of thing *real* sailors knew.

Half-an-hour later, somewhere upstairs towards the back of the same building, I unlocked the door to a newly-refurbished single room with an ensuite. It was just within my budget. The embossed cream-coloured wallpaper looked handsome, the bed was comfortable. Sumptuous dark carpet was magic to my feet, which had been enclosed in steel-capped shoes for most of the previous 14 days.

There was a restaurant downstairs with rotating five-pound specials. I could stay for as long as I needed.

By then I'd discovered the property's guests — of whom there seemed few — were likely current and ex-members (and their families) of the Royal and Merchant Navy, the Royal Marines, and the Armed Forces.

You got lucky, girl!

At work, thousands of Euros went through the ferry tills each trip: mini towers of alcohol hauled to cars; perfume shoved in handbags. Several crew said to me in my first two weeks, "No one comes *from* cruise ships, *to* ferries — it goes the other way!"

That first night in the Royal Sailors' Home Club, there was no time to dream of the perpetually-open shop. I closed my eyes — *I just need a good night's sl*— and dropped into the abyss.

14

T he young man — whom I guessed was a few years older than me, in his late twenties — had issued the invitation several weeks earlier, during our shoreside training for the cross-Channel ferries. After most of the fire-fighting, survival at sea and maritime theory was finished, he'd said: "My parents have a seven-bedroom house over on the Isle of Wight, you should come and visit."

I liked his voice and the way his smile filled his eyes. He had fine hands and long eyelashes.

The Isle of Wight was a 25-minute ferry ride across The Solent from Portsmouth, and like somewhere out of a children's book of English bedtime stories. The young man and I walked up the hill from the dock in Ryde. We meandered to a square rimmed by neat Victorian houses and opened a red door with the number 9 on it.

He made me a cup of tea and we settled in the living room. I could hear others upstairs. He said they'd likely be down soon.

"Dad, this is Sara," he said, trying to catch the attention of a man in the hallway, just near the living room door.

I was sitting at the table, with my back to the door. I turned to see a bearded man, looking down at something he was holding — some sort of tool, from memory — then getting very cross and cursing. He ignored us.

"Dad!"

"What?!" He spun in the direction of the voice, peering over his glasses that had slid a little down his nose.

"I said, this is Sara. She's working on the ferries too."

"Oh, it's Sara this week, is it?"

The man gave me the briefest of dismissive glances before returning to his momentary fury about however he was being thwarted.

That was how I met my father-in-law to be.

————

The young man's mother was the kind and calming influence in a family with six mostly-grown children. As I remember it, the youngest, towards the end of high school, was still at home there on the Isle of Wight; the eldest was married and gone; and the four in between were all in various stages of coming and going. They were English — with roots in the North — but all fluent in French as they'd lived between England and France for years.

A chaotic and tantalising household, arguments could erupt at any moment. Often a disagreement would kick off while several of us were brewing cups of Earl Grey tea at the wooden kitchen table fit for war room planning — and moments later, amid vocal sound effects and a volley of deprecating in-jokes, everyone would be doubled over laughing.

The house always had the faint smell of fresh washing and home cooking, or sometimes, when the renovations were moving along, fresh paint.

My first meeting of the father aside, the family welcomed me. And continued to do so after an unexpected event.

The young man said casually one day while we were staying over for the weekend at his parents' place, "My brother's coming over from France in a couple of weeks — you should come and meet him."

So I did.

I was at the front door when the man arrived from France, got out of his car, smiled and said hello. And in that instant, I thought: *Oh shit, I'm with the wrong brother.*

————

The two brothers and I went to the pub for lunch that day. I had my hand on the leg of one, while becoming besotted with the other.

"You should come and visit," said the brother-from-France, to me.

Uh-oh.

"Sure, that would be great!" I replied. *Too enthusiastic, Sara.* "Though don't invite me unless you really mean it, because I will take you up on that offer," I added.

He raised his eyebrows and smiled just before he drank from his pint glass; it looked like an I-wouldn't-ask-you-if-I-didn't-mean-it sort of expression.

"Well, I've plans for my next shore leave; maybe the break after that," I said, trying to sound off-hand and not compound my growing awkwardness.

The brother-from-France became The Englishman I couldn't get out of my head. Clearly the young man and I had to part ways.

————

After a 12-hour shift in the shop on the ferry, I escaped to the deck and the remnants of a sunset. It was serene. Soundless, aside from the wash of our bow wave; I no longer heard the engine growl. Deep smoky-blue clouds hid the sun and a strip of fluorescent pink highlighted the horizon. When I squinted slightly, it was possible to completely lose the definition between sea and sky.

I briefly slipped out of my stiff shoes and let my stocking-covered feet rest on the metal floor as I leaned on the railing. I undid the top button on my navy-coloured waistcoat and rolled the sleeves of my white blouse to my elbows. My red, yellow and royal blue scarf remained neatly tucked below my collar, its flourish draped above the buttons of my blouse.

Rolling my shoulders, I tried and failed to appease the knotted muscles between my shoulder blades: receive money across counter, put money into till, return change; repeat.

During the death throes of the day, beyond the blue cloud bank there was a world ablaze with crimson light. We could have been sailing upon a lake; only a few boats dotted the scene, illuminated against the dimming sky. The boats appeared to be right at the horizon — at the edge of the world. The place I always wanted to go.

What's over there?

15

France. Northern France. Normandy. My first impression of you — while I was with The Englishman for the first time, in the passenger seat of his van — was a sound: *kerthunk, kerthunk, kerthunk*. Hundreds of tyres rolled off the metal gangway onto asphalt at the Port of Le Havre.

He drove the two of us into your interior. Your yet-to-be-familiar otherness descended. Your road signs bore new combinations of consonants, vowels and inflections. The font was different to the signs of England, too. Your trees and fields configured themselves with another geometry, though I couldn't say *exactly* how they were different.

Euros bloomed in my purse and my Great British Pounds were tucked away in a pocket of my little red bag with orange lining.

———

Early morning travel wasn't my friend; a prickly perspiration gripped me, even though it was cold. As the sun forged higher in the sky, I tried to keep my nausea at bay and my eyes open after a long work week shunting to-and-fro across the English Channel.

The Englishman and I looked out for *gendarmes* on the motorway. No flashing lights pursued us. As the road blurred into a few hours, I snatched increasingly longer micro sleeps. I emerged from a deep instant nap with a start that was hard to disguise.

I hope he's not an axe murderer...a bit late now, if so...

The motorway had been traded for a minor road, a 'B-road', as I learned the British said.

I actually have no idea where I am.

But isn't that half the fun?

Let's hope so.

I ate my first fresh-baked *pain au chocolat* from a *boulangerie* in a tiny village that morning; the clutch of stone houses unchanged since...I didn't know when. I tried to contain the unruly scatterings of fine golden pastry. They rained further beyond my lap with each bite. I wiped their tiny fragments from the edges of my lips while savouring the sweet confection of the chocolate laced at the pastry's centre. A chocolate that was instantly in all of my mouth.

France, I will eat you.

The Englishman chuckled at my efforts and had a brief chat with the locals, who were buying their bread for lunch; his switch between English and French was swift and apparently effortless. He stood at least 30 centimetres (one foot) taller than all of them, with an air of geniality. Later he would tell me people in France often thought he was Belgian.

We arrived at the rural property near Savigny-le-Vieux, from which he and his father came and went as their reclaimed timber flooring business required.

"So, you can sleep upstairs here," The Englishman said as he opened the door to a book-lined cottage, a *gite,* with a fireplace, simple couch and dining table; kitchen in the back corner. "Make yourself comfortable downstairs too, of course."

I put my bag by the double bed in the loft, noted the European-size pillows — *another thing that's different here* — and re-emerged into the daylight.

"Where will you be?" I asked.

He pointed a few dozen metres across the yard to some sort of out building: "It used to be a bread oven. We still call it that. I've just put a new floor in."

"Oh yeah? Do I get to see it?"

There were so many pieces of timber underfoot in a relatively small space — like thick, headless matchsticks laid end to end, wrought and marked by time but still characterful. I was familiar with the appreciation of knots and grain and line; my Dad had co-owned and run a timber mill on our farm. The Englishman had a similar vocabulary for his admiration and a look I'd seen before, as he told me about the construction.

"I'm surprised you're interested," The Englishman said, "in the floor."

"I'm full of surprises," I smiled.

His blue eyes crinkled under his wavy blonde-brown hair and he flashed a broad grin.

I see you.

For three days, we had birds, cows and sunshine for company. I cobbled together a dinner the first night from meagre ingredients in the cupboards; chicken, onions, pasta and some sort of packet sauce, I think. He waited weeks before confiding he hated onions.

"What would you like to do?" The Englishman asked, mid-morning of another clear-sky day. "Do you want to see Mont-Saint-Michel?"

I'd never heard of the storied stone abbey he described,

perched high on a hill, beyond the coast at high tide and surrounded by sea for part of each day.

Walking amid tourists on the cobblestoned road spiralling heavenwards, Mont-Saint-Michel was the Middle Ages, kept alive. Within its walls, I looked back towards land from a narrow window in the rock; sun blazed across the shallows and the water became a silver sequinned swathe, deepening the terrestrial shadows.

The two of us browsed an exhibition in the monastery.

Is it obvious, I wonder, that I'm only half-able to take in anything right now? Do I make him feel like this too? I'd better think of something sensible to say.

I snatched a glance at The Englishman.

He'd sometimes brush his hand across my back as he walked to another display; the detaching again, an exquisite little pain.

"So, as part of my round-the-world plane ticket, I have a flight to Rome. Would you like to take a short break in Italy with me?"

And there it was. My invitation issued mostly to a painting, also swirling in the centimetres between us as we stood side by side; eye contact for the final few words. My swift addition: "No pressure. I mean, we've only known each other for—"

"I'd like that," The Englishman said. And we both looked at the painting in silence for a little while.

He showed me the cottage ruin he owned, about 20 minutes' drive from the *gite*. All I could see in the bones of the place was possibility.

That evening, he lit the fire and we talked into the night, mingling confidences with the longest kiss.

16

S omehow I managed to sleep in my cabin as the Channel raged. I woke from my usual split-shift nap and knew there was trouble. The winter storm had not abated — it was probably worse than when I lay down a couple of hours earlier. White angry waves, up to 12 metres (40 feet), squalled at my large porthole that was usually much further above sea level.

But that wasn't why I thought there was something wrong. It was the 'no signal' indicator on my mobile phone. We should have sailed back into the range of the towers on England's South Coast by that time of day. So we were still a long way from shore.

If we are still a long way out, we're sailing very slowly.

I hoped it was only due to bad weather.

I took off my pyjamas and donned layer on layer of uniform, lifting each item in turn off the back of the chair at my desk. Thankful the person in the cabin next door hadn't forgotten to unlock my side of our two-way bathroom.

This is like hurricane territory. But we're tiny compared to my first cruise ship.

Ricocheting gently from surface to surface as I prepared for

the remainder of my shift in the shop, I hoped I'd get to
stay there.

As the ferry had begun to bob and sway into gale force winds
earlier that morning, I was sent below decks to tally inventory.
There was a blood-in-your-mouth smell down there in the stuffy
storeroom. Bilious, with a clipboard in hand, it wasn't long
before I abandoned the task of counting and logging stock, and
returned to the shop via my cabin bathroom.

*When you have your face in the toilet bowl this early in the day,
it's really time to rethink your work choices, Sara.*

In the next breath: *Just a few more weeks now. Hold on.*

I'd had sleep and food since then and, though I couldn't
right my body, my stomach wasn't threatening to expel its
contents anymore.

Until I got up on deck again and smelled the vomit. Not all
passengers had the luxury of a cabin. Sometimes the foot
passengers booked only a chair for the almost-five-hour crossing
— and too bad if the person next to them became greener by the
minute. It wasn't an option to go outside. The gates of Hades had
opened out there.

The shop was shut.

I had to bang on the fireproof door. One of my colleagues
stuck her head out gingerly to check I wasn't an enraged ticket
holder, and let me in. I was shocked by the transformation of the
place. Everyone else was shocked I'd managed to sleep.

It's my defence mechanism.

Whole stand-alone displays of beer, wine and spirits had
toppled and smashed, with more stock careening off the shelves
with each wave, into the sodden glass-splintered carpet. The
perfume displays had become a liquid mess too — though a
more fragrant one — and there was a graveyard of mannequins
dressed in leisurewear, pointing at the ceiling.

The mop up had been done and the passengers had been

locked out for a while. I'd entered the 'cling film apocalypse'. All remaining stock had been wrapped in cling film and then wrapped onto its shelf. Anything else that could fall down had been taken down.

Even the crew on shift — about five of us — were sitting on the floor in the middle of it all. I think the others played cards at one point. There was nothing to do but wait it out. I was oddly calm.

Until I heard there was a malfunction with one of the engines so we were cut to half-power. Until it became known we were taking on water on one of the car decks. Until it seemed a helicopter couldn't rescue any of us if we needed it because the weather was too bad.

"So, we're slowly sinking as we're limping back to Portsmouth?" I asked.

"Yes. Just don't tell the passengers. We've given out food vouchers," someone said.

Well, that's okay then! We'd better bloody make it. I refuse to die in the middle of the English fucking Channel.

I'd told The Englishman on the phone about our awful crossing; how it had taken us *12 hours* to get back to Portsmouth; how we were the *only* ferry to sail the Channel that day, in what turned out to be a Force 10 storm.

"I heard the forecast. That was madness; I thought of you. So, about tomorrow: I'll come straight off the ferry from France and pick you up from the sailors' club. See you about 6am," he said.

Around 5.45am, I pulled my long-sleeved maroon top a little further below the waist of my navy-coloured bootleg jeans. I did a quick front-to-back twirl — grateful for the jeans castoff

from Charlotte, and that Samantha had taken me on an
'emergency' trip to Topshop when it had become apparent the
clothing I'd brought in my backpack wasn't going to keep me
from the cold.

Looking good.

Despite the unholy hour, I was deliciously clean and happy. I
just had to put on lip gloss then give my blow-dried hair a quick
final comb; it was getting long, almost down to my bra clasp.

Tripping off to London with my new man. Fancy that.

It hit again. That feeling I'd had en route to my first ship;
again in New York. Milder echoes had come since, including
when The Englishman and I had first gone to Normandy.

What's wrong with me?

I dashed to the bathroom and was ill. Bile and empty-
stomach saliva was bitter in my mouth. Perspiration erupted and
a feverish shaking gripped me as I feared being late and my eyes
watered as my stomach constricted again.

How can I go anywhere like this? I need to try and eat something.

At the thought of food, my senses shut down. Overload.
Then the diarrhoea began. The clock ticked on. I was going to
be late.

Downstairs in the deserted lobby soon after, I sucked on a
peppermint as I assembled a brave face atop a re-cleaned and
scented body. The Englishman pulled up and I left my haven
and went into the dark cold and got in the passenger seat of his
transit van. He leaned over and kissed me. My body was
rebelling.

"Wait a minute," he said, "I need to rearrange some of the
stuff in the back before we go."

I can't do this. I need the bathroom again.

*No, you'll be fine. There's nothing left inside you. Think of
something else.*

It's a long drive to London, I don't know if I...

"Hey, I've just got to duck to the bathroom, I'll be back in a sec," I said into the back of the van, not waiting for a reply.

I held my own hair back as I wretched into the bowl. I was grateful the toilets were clean and I wasn't in some service station restroom.

Small mercies. Come on, get it together, time to go, he's waiting for you.

Getting back into the van, I said, "Right, London here we come!"

"Are you okay? Your eyes are wild."

"I'm fine. Let's get going."

––––––––

As I emerged from the shopping centre in the heart of Portsmouth, I briefly suspected I was the butt of some elaborate prank.

How can it be dark already? It's only 4.15pm...

Of course, it was just winter and I only *truly* realised it at that moment: as I finished my Christmas shopping for The Englishman and his family, and stood gawping at the black sky in mild shock, holding several gifts yet to be wrapped.

Winter at Christmas. No dripping heat, salads and pavlova here. My first Christmas like the movies; and the cards with snowflakes and carol singers with cheeks bright from cold.

I needed some rest after a frenetic year during which I'd rarely been in one place for more than a week.

Festivities on the Isle of Wight wouldn't herald any quiet but that was okay. I had a small pang thinking of what I was missing while on the phone to Mum and Dad on Christmas morning, but it dissipated.

About 12 of us — The Englishman's parents, grandma, siblings and their partners — stuffed ourselves with great rolling, teasing conversation at the decorated table nobly bearing the weight of roast meats and vegetables and Yorkshire pudding.

"Eat up, Sara, you'll fade away even further; have some more!"

Half the tipsy crowd stumbled into the post-lunch frigid air for a fanciful England v. Australia game of cricket. I had to recruit a few helpers for that one. Dessert, gifts and board games by the open fire rounded out the short afternoon.

Before a nap curled me into the sofa, I smiled into my drowsiness — the memories of Italy had been coming in little vignettes during the previous weeks since I'd returned.

The Englishman and I had been on the train from Rome to Venice forever; the countryside a backdrop to the melodrama aboard. Everyone wanted to sit where we were but we'd stood for a long time in the narrow aisle and seized our chance at seats opposite each other in a bank of four, after we realised there weren't really any allocations. Despite what the ticket seller had said. The train was just the moving whirl of the street.

*Rome, we've just been wandering on holiday **in Rome**! Even though you missed your flight — I can't stay mad at you for long. You got here. We got to the Colosseum and Roman Forum and Trevi Fountain and all the other places the tourists are mad for, but I didn't care because it was **Rome** and you and me.*

A feisty English-South African lady chatted with us on the train for a while, fancying herself a bit of a clairvoyant.

"You two will be back here for your honeymoon, I just know it!"

The carriage rolled gently, and stop-started violently at each station; my knees knocked and brushed against The Englishman's in a strange percussive dance. We pushed northwards, Venice in its half-drowned majesty and decay, in the darkness ahead...

And now it was Christmas.

I looked over the small pile of carefully-chosen gifts I had received, and replayed the apparent delight prompted by those I'd given too. But I was most excited by one I couldn't open: a small classified ad I'd answered in the back of *Wanderlust* magazine a few months earlier, was about to work its magic.

What do you have for me, 2003? I can't wait. I'll see you soon, shining new year.

17

Austria. Alpine wonder. In January, I dipped into your white unknown amid my own flurry of hot excitement — a wanderer with a mission across your high altitudes.

I did not know what I'd find, in the shifts of your atmospheres, amid the rock and snow; on valley floors; in the conversations bubbling into the sky. I was yet to glide in the hum on your autobahn: a daredevil playground.

You were my first. The first of many solo trips that way: a foreign airport to a foreign town, in a car I'd never driven before — on an itinerary of someone else's making. I had a map. I had a layering of resistance and resilience; momentum and desire.

Whatever happened, there was always desire.

———

Most of my fellow passengers were tourists en route to the Tyrolean ski fields. I marvelled at the peaks pushing above the clouds, until our plane dipped at an alarming angle; mountain-rimmed Innsbruck somewhere below. We landed

into about −8 degrees C (17 degrees F); my hands and pen
freezing as I attempted my hire car paperwork outside, by
the car.

Driving into the mountains — climbing, twisting — my left
hand kept hitting the driver's side door as I went to change gear;
my brain yet to adjust to a left-hand drive on the right. My heart
snapped a double-time beat when I first encountered the signs
warning about the possible need for chains.

I've only been to the snow once. A school excursion for a week
when I was 16. But this is not like Jindabyne. What the hell do I do
with snow chains? Are there any in the car now? How are they fitted?
When do you need them? I really should have done more research...

For a while I gripped the steering wheel like it was my life
source. Perspiration beaded underneath my jacket because I
daren't take my eyes off the road to work out how to adjust the
then-tropical heating.

All I could see as I arrived into Seefeld, on a low cloud
afternoon with darkness hovering, was a large village which
only had snow cleared from its main road.

Oh man — how can I tell where the other roads are now?

I crawled the car across what I hoped were the right places,
and not through someone's garden, as I searched for my bed-
and-breakfast, desperate to just stop. I only peeled my hands
from the steering wheel and fully exhaled once I was safely
parked in the tiny courtyard of my accommodation.

Snow fell during the night. Everyone awoke to the buzz
brought by clear skies and fresh powder.

When I'd emailed Nick at sea, to tell him my first trip was to
Austria, he was horrified I had to spend two weeks in prime
season without the chance to go skiing. All I knew about skiing
was that I couldn't stop when I started and that would be
problematic given the size of the peaks around me. No, I was
content to walk the villages everyone else cabled out of — up, up

and away, in pursuit of their perfect descent. I had a clipboard
and a job to do.

———

I was officially spoiled for backpacking in about 20 seconds.
That was how long it took for a doorman to grip a brass handle
on a tall wooden door and usher me and my snowy boots onto
the plush red carpet of the foyer of the five-star Hotel
Klosterbräu.

Klosterbräu was the epitome of sumptuousness and
elegance I'd only read about in travel magazines. As I sat on a
velvet bench seat, just off to the side of the reception area, I
could see a book-lined room with dark green curtains and deep
leather armchairs by a well-tended open fire. People in the
lobby moved with the grace and charm of the perpetually
unhurried. The staff were dressed immaculately.

I removed my jacket — the warmest I had, but a couple of
sizes too big — purchased from a friend at a surf shop several
years earlier. After corralling stray hairs back into my ponytail, I
removed a questionnaire from the laptop bag I was carrying, put
it inside my clipboard folder, grabbed a business card and made
my way towards reception.

Shoulders back, stand straight. Smile.

"Hello, my name is Sara, and I'm reviewing hotels for the UK
travel guide, *Gazetteers*. I'd like to ask you a few brief questions
about the property," I said.

"You are from where?" the stony receptionist asked, ignoring
the card I'd placed on the counter between us.

"*Gazetteers*. It includes reviews of about 13,000 hotels and
800 resorts worldwide. This won't take long."

"We do not pay to be included in that."

"Oh no, this isn't a paid review, your property is included

because there are many guests who come here from Britain," I said as I opened my clipboard, "and I just need to confirm a few details and check if anything has changed since Klosterbräu was last visited by one of our writers."

"We are very busy. We do not have time for this."

"If I could just have a brochure—"

Dismissed.

Hmmm. Okay, this is going to be a bit harder than I thought.

The budget accommodation, a few streets but many worlds away from Klosterbräu, made its impression indelible by festooning all the common areas with greenery. I'd never seen so many plants indoors. It was like stepping into an alpine nursery that served food.

Its elevated front terrace also served a stunning view: a cluster of thick-timbered, broad-roofed shops and chateaux, so resolute and sturdy on a human scale but dwarfed by indomitable peaks pressed close around them. Everyone was friendly. A joyful murmur of background conversation rippled across the sunny hotel terrace.

"May I have a hot chocolate, please?" I asked the waitress from my little corner table, looking out across the village.

"Yes, of course. Would you like anything else?"

"Hmm, a croissant thanks."

I unzipped my jacket a little. Icicles hanging from the edge of the roof were melting into the late morning, radiant little prisms of water dripped their own rhythm onto the dirty snow slush at the building's edge; the slopes were pristine. Complete satisfaction engulfed me.

This is fantastic. I'm getting paid to be here!

The brush off at the first hotel that morning had thrown me initially, but the complete lack of interest in my presence was a favour: I'd looked around the common areas on my own, surreptitiously taking notes, and waited until I could talk to a

different receptionist to confirm details and pick up a new
brochure. At the subsequent properties, I'd begun my practice of
trying to blend in in any hotel public space — or at the very
least, not stand out.

It's a six-month contract; I'm sure I'll work it out as I go along.

As I ate, I imagined the first half of the year bubbling with
mystery destinations I'd visit. Only the sweep of geography was
known, reflecting the volumes issued across the publication
schedule: ski, lakes and mountains; long haul; North America;
European cities; Mediterranean.

My thoughts flicked back to the group interview in London
and the impromptu speech we all had to give about why we
wanted the job.

*The company reps had all taken notice when I said I was
currently working 84-hour weeks on the ferries. When I said I wasn't
afraid of hard work.*

I circled the hotels to visit that afternoon in green on my
map, and set out again. Head high, back straight. Ridiculous
grin.

As I put my sunglasses over their white space on my red face
the next morning, I chided myself: *You only need 'snowburn' once
to learn **that** lesson, eh?*

Just before I left Seefeld, I walked to the edge of town. The
sun, snow and cloudless sky were all dazzling; all silent. I
inhaled deeply, slowly.

*This is what the air near the top of the world smells like: hollow...
sharp...pure. It's cleaning me as I breathe.*

All the peaks etched their own signature into the skyline, the
rock and shadows and snow drifts playing light tricks well above
the trees.

I could live here.

———

Early on a winter's evening — in the pregnant space after rudimentary unpacking at a new hotel, but before I'd decided what to do next — I sat on a white cotton bedspread in my wood-panelled room that resembled a sauna.

Perhaps I should have enjoyed the last place a little more.

A company-issued laptop sat on the small desk, awaiting input from the morning's hotel visits — spreadsheets that would accumulate in the file list of 16 reviews I'd already written during the first couple of days away.

Brimming with discoveries, I dialled a London number.

"Hey, it's me! How are you, hon?" I said when Naomi answered her phone. She'd left cruise ships and moved to the UK too. So much had happened in 18 months since we'd been at sea together. She and Charlotte and I saw each other whenever we could.

"Hi! Are you back already?" Naomi asked.

"Nope, hi from Austria! From the snow. It's amazing and I wanted to talk to you."

"Oh, honey, you're lonely."

"No, I'm fine. Well, yeah — a bit."

Before we hung up, Naomi said, "Love you!" and it warmed me in the cold.

It was too early to call Australia. I tried The Englishman again with the remainder of my calling card balance: it still went to voicemail.

———

Australia's mountains are ancient, well-worn low rise affairs. *Austria's* are young, sharp and imposing by comparison.

I shot into a tunnel through a mountain. My shriek of delight rocketed as sensors in the car detected a loss of light and illuminated the whole dash.

"Wow, it's all red!"

And I was piloting an intergalactic starship navigating a frozen outer world.

Bam! Out of the tunnel again and midday sun smashed into my eyes and the car was stark and I was snaking a black line heading to the bottom of a valley, with walls of snow-covered rock heaving skywards.

"Woooooooohooooooo! Austria! Yeah!"

————

No après ski crowd jostled at the bar near my room, spinning off laughter and spent delight from a day on the slopes. I couldn't revel vicariously in their holiday banter — all smatterings of German, French, Italian, Spanish, English — glad of the people nearby, like I'd done several days earlier in Obergurgl.

No, Telfs was a silent little place of mist and snowfall. The skeletons of trees dusting in and out of view as I fogged up the big picture window of my loft apartment with my breath, watching the snow globe world beyond.

Don't wish away time, Sara.

It was the end of my two-week trip. Those 14 days seemed to compress another half-lifetime within them — and it would feel that way on every successive occasion.

I'd made countless footprints in the snow in the chateaux-dotted towns on my itinerary. Maps and distances had been checked and double-checked. Scores of hotel reviews and brochures were neatly paper-clipped together in manila envelopes in my backpack. A USB stick with the digital versions of the reviews was in my hand luggage.

My Christmas gift copy of Alain de Botton's *The Art of Travel* sat bookmarked on the coffee table.

I was fidgety. There was only so much small-talk with

strangers I could make. Friends were busy. I thought Mum would worry if I called too often.

Hello from over here, again!

The Englishman seemed to spin away and I couldn't quite reach him, even when my phone call made it through. And what would I say to him? 'I miss you' — again. Saying it once had already felt like enough.

That last night of my first time in Austria, I sang in the oversized shower, all the notes steaming into the mist inside; trying to shift the melancholy that had settled upon me just as softly as the snowflakes had been falling on the ridge all afternoon.

18

The Dominican Republic. You startled me. I thought I knew you because I'd been to the Caribbean before. But before, I'd only really dropped in for lunch; on other islands, with other histories.

This time, a skip-jump airstrip landing amid a storm had begun my work trip, and its trajectory faltered on. Into your six-lane highway near the capital — rife with cars, scooters, animals, pedestrians. All laden with life but cheating death at each turn, intersection and traffic lights. I somehow drove through the honking morass, invoking an atheist's prayer.

You were a place half wrought from jungle; sloughing off your vegetation and preening a new patina.

My itinerary pushed into the chasm between your five-star resorts with soaring iron gates, and your huts next door to them: electricity optional.

And I found you shared your island with a shadow. Would Haiti ever come to the ball?

One February day in the Dominican Republic I turned 25. It was 2003.

I'd befriended a few holidaying Canadians by the pool of the hotel at which we were all staying. One of them was a silversmith.

"It's your birthday, you've gotta have something," he said as he handed me a ring he'd made — one that he'd been wearing earlier — while I blushed. His friends were talking at the pool bar.

"That's really kind of you but I can't take that," I said, thinking of the canary-yellow walled apartment in south-west London that I'd moved into with The Englishman and his best mate, just after Christmas.

"Why not?" the silversmith's question was genuine.

"You...made it for you," was all I spluttered, not wanting to deflate the kind gesture.

I'd delighted in simply washing clothes and hanging them in the wardrobe next to The Englishman's. He worked in France while I was away and aimed to be home in Wandsworth when I was.

"I'd like you to have it. Really. Happy birthday," the silversmith said, beaming.

He's being nice. It doesn't mean anything if you accept it. That's probably the polite thing to do.

"Thank you," I smiled. It only fit on my thumb but I wore it for several days.

"Hey, we're all going to a baseball match in town tonight — do you wanna come?"

I wanted the night off typing up reviews. I wanted to feel part of a group. I didn't want to spend my first night being 25, alone.

"Okay, great."

"Meet you out the front of the hotel at seven."

So I cheered with Canadians in rickety wooden stands for a

Dominican team playing an American sport, while I was a long way from home. And I'd never have picked it or planned it, but it felt right.

I rode that high as I traced my way across the country on a 10-hour drive. On a deserted stretch north of Punta Cana, I took a table one mid-afternoon at a small newly-built hotel and looked at the breaking waves on the beach about 20 metres (65 feet) away. Sprite effervesced on my tongue and it wasn't quite as sweet as I remembered. I'd refused ice. I contemplated ordering a burger but the kitchen was about to close. My stomach growled.

I wonder if this is the beginning for this place. If 2003 will be when the tourists started to come. If this will be the last time there's just one hotel here — near nothing else.

Later: *two flat tyres in 13 days, really travel gods?*

On each occasion — once in a hotel car park, and once at a service station in the middle of nowhere — I'd hoped, hands vaguely ringing and stomach a little knotted, that the men helping me would be satisfied with only my sincere thanks; with the gratitude I mimed and my '*gracias, muchas gracias señor*'. I drove away quickly each time, feeling a dash of good luck had come after bad.

There had been one phrase in the accommodation column of my itinerary staring at me for the whole trip but I'd thought nothing of it: 'Own arrangements'. It was to give me the freedom to choose where to break my return journey for the night, on my haul back to Puerto Plata and my departing flight.

Eating up the highway, micro-sleeps began to lull my consciousness.

Dangerous, Sara.

I'll stop in the next town.

But the next town seemed too small. I pushed on for another hour or so, window down, singing out loud, drinking cold water and splashing it on my face — doing all the things the road accident ads said wouldn't help the weary driver cheat death.

I pulled off the highway into a large village and stopped to fish out my library copy of Lonely Planet's *Dominican Republic,* and looked up the town: "Do not stay here unless you have absolutely no choice. All tourists are advised to keep driving."

About six men had already taken an interest in my car and were ambling towards me. All the times I'd wandered on my own in back streets of the world — just looking, taking photos — came to mind: a dense flip book it was, too. In that instant, I sensed how much luck I'd already used. Ignition on.

Damn. Wakey-wakey. Here we go again.

The weird-smelling, side-of-the-road motel room I found myself in that night had its brightest bulb in the wardrobe. I curled myself behind the cupboard's louvred doors — that I'd opened as far as I could — into a half-foetal position and balanced my laptop awkwardly on my knees to finish writing up my reviews. I had a Cup-a-Soup for dinner.

Oh, the glamour.

Just before I fell asleep on the lumpy mattress, I was grateful I couldn't see the detail of the grotty decor and hoped: a) the lock on my door would hold, and b) I would never again have to pick my own accommodation while working.

————

My body had warmed and loosened again in the Caribbean. The snap back to a bitter London February morning was jarring; bristling. The Englishman was due to meet my 6.30am flight but he wasn't there. I waited a little while at the gate before I went to baggage claim. I waited longer at baggage claim. He wasn't answering his phone.

Perhaps, subconsciously, I still felt nervous at reuniting or my mind conjured all sorts of disaster-reasons as to why he wasn't there. I don't know. But the disorienting nausea began; the mental flicker that all was not well.

No, not now.

It kicked my instincts into overdrive.

Home. I just need to get home.

I followed the signs to the train; checked the timetable at the platform. My fear of not being in the right place nagging and welling.

I should wait. Are there toilets on the train? If I wait, I don't know how I'll go in the car whenever he does arrive. Thanks for picking me up, here, let me vomit on you.

Still no answer to my texts or voicemails.

I boarded the next train from Gatwick and texted The Englishman to tell him so. I went straight to bed when I got home: hoping the wooziness would disappear, wondering where my boyfriend was, realising just how weary I was as I pulled the lavender-coloured quilt up around my shoulders.

The Englishman threw his coat on the bed sometime after 9.30am. I stirred quickly.

"Where were you? I waited and called and in the end just had to get home so I caught the train," I said.

"I was in traffic, I got there just after you landed — there's no signal in the car park, by the way — and you were gone. I got stuck in peak hour on the way home again."

"I'm so sorry."

He produced a single rose from inside his coat. I'd been away for my birthday and Valentine's Day.

"I was going to give you this at the airport," he said, "it's no use now." He tossed it on the floor and left the room.

I shrivelled at a homecoming lost.

We were heavy-footed for a while, stepping in and out of each other's space while also trying to make one together.

19

Each passport stamp was a hieroglyphic, holding the impending or unfolded moments within a week or two. Their different inks, fonts and languages — impressed neatly or crowding in on each other — had a haphazard chronology. Flip pages forward; flip back. Sometimes the stamp was marked in pen, an extra flourish from an immigration official who always bore the first impression of a place. But after a while, I discovered, not necessarily a reliable one. Those officials usually resembled each other more than their nation.

While I researched and reviewed hotels, the thwack of the passport entry stamp was a kill switch. Home week: done. Gone was the re-acquainting with The Englishman, skin to skin; apologies and dreams breathed between us into the darkness, his warm-bodied company in early light. Over was the lunch with friends. Lost was the day to buses and the Tube and overland trains to the office and back — hand over files, pick up new plane tickets. Paused was the administration of life and the endless washing, drying and re-packing.

The thwack of the passport entry stamp was also the lights

going on in another stadium. Over and over: let the games
begin.

———

Ansel Adams had been a hero to my photography class. His
moody black and white images of Yosemite National Park were
lauded. While I drove, I reconciled my memory of his work with
my glimpses of the granite peaks above the black oak and
ponderosa pine trees. His images were linked to my learning —
practising black and white printing by hand. The tang of
remembered chemical trays was at the back of my throat:
developer, wash, fixer.

Long stretches slipped under my wheels in Yosemite and I
rarely saw a soul — not by rivers, at camp grounds nor on the
other side of hard bends.

I pulled over and stared into a stream rippling with golden
afternoon light. I waited. Nothing. I scanned the ridges and
mountains. Nothing.

*Maybe I'm missing the Ansel Adams thing — that essence he
captured — because I'm really just thinking about bears. There are
warning signs everywhere. Bears have a good sense of smell. Can they
smell fear? That ranger wasn't exactly comforting when I drove in the
gate this morning. I s'pose they get sick of tourists taking it lightly...*

Onwards.

About a week later, in March sun in a waterfront park in
Monterey, California, I added to my mental journal of scavenged
facts and impressions from everywhere I'd been.

Amid picnicking families, and old couples on park benches
looking out to the pristine sea, I came to know Spanish settlers
first arrived on the coast there in 1769. I imagined pilgrims,
soldiers and explorers establishing new missions, forts and
settlements — bringing their gods, customs and architecture to

'Alta California'. A sign in the park also informed me that the region once belonged to Mexico (after Mexico won independence from Spain). After the discovery of gold in 1850, California became a US state.

Australia was on the opposite shore of the ocean laid sparkling before me. I was roughly halfway between London and Brisbane. Both had pieces of me. I looked to the horizon and felt the internal tug in opposite directions; like the bubble of a spirit level that never quite steadied within the lines.

I confess my heart is always in more than one place.

I walked back towards my hotel, which took me past the local cinema. One poster snapped my attention. The independent award-winning film *Rabbit-Proof Fence* was showing. I sat in America and watched three young girls trek 2,400 kilometres (1,500 miles) through Australia's vast interior, trying to reunite with their Aboriginal family.

And there, in the dark, hot tears ran down my face. I volleyed a fierce-burning flare across the Pacific to Mum.

I hope you get this, Ma, that you know how much I love you. How I always will. I miss you but you gave me the greatest gift you could by letting me go away again. Without fuss, without telling me any of your fears, only encouraging me with your hopes. Though it would be so nice if you were here now...

It was a fireball to unite kindreds across space and time. A flint for its light in my very bones. And I knew in that instant our bond could never be extinguished, no matter where we were.

———

In April, US troops tore down the statue of Saddam Hussein in Firdos Square, central Baghdad.

Those jets are hunters.

Half the crowd cheered; others bayed for blood. More blood.

I watched on BBC World from my hotel room in Marbella, on the south coast of Spain, and it all felt a little too close for comfort. I was accustomed to all the strife being half a world away.

That evening, the theatrics and merriment that was a street full of Spanish diners at 10pm were a comfort.

———

I had no idea how hemmed in I'd felt in London, until everything was gone from view. Until the landscape looked Martian. Until I was the slingshot between road, rock and the sky on an outcrop in the Atlantic; Africa brooding far behind me.

As I gathered speed on Fuerteventura, all my junk thoughts and sorrows just flew away. All the 'noise' evaporated into the clear air on that Canary Island that was so far from anything else.

That release was part of my addiction; part of the desire for momentum. But I didn't realise it for a long time.

Caleta de Fuste was a tiny coastal enclave of low rise buildings. There were hostels, apartments, a couple of bars with lobster-red Englishmen and deep-tanned blonde German girls. I guessed the couple of restaurants would be rowdiest around 11pm — relying on alcohol to infuse them with atmosphere so no one noticed the basic fare. A dive shop near the waterfront traded on the promise of an aqua sea adventure.

My tiled apartment was all gleaming white and a bit too cool because it wasn't quite summer. All my rushing: property after property, town after town, country after country — it was a frenetic, high-strung haven.

What do you think will happen if you stop?

I sat on the balcony and looked at the wide palette of

nothingness before me. With every moment that was vacant, I was restored.

Down south in Jandia, where the havoc of the wind was a good thing, where the world kitesurfing championships had been held since 1984, I stood at the railing of a hotel rooftop with my hair flying and looked across the sea. Behind me, bikini girls tried to look casual by the pool; young muscle men strutted. The aroma of coconut oil seeped into all of us. Then, as if someone spoke softly into my ear:

You know, this time will never come again.

The next morning, in the snug stillness of my very comfortable hotel room — with a view to the white-tipped mess of an ocean; to the bending palm trees with rasping pom-poms of greenery — I gradually pushed all work out of my day. I tried to be leisurely about it.

'You have time off once all your chores are done,' came my father's voice to my small self, neck craned. Surely he was a giant.

*This time will never come again. What do **you** want to do?*

In a pale green armchair, in fits and starts — restless and admonishing, then calm — I devoured a novel. Until it was dark.

And I laughed at the insignificance of my rebellion.

———

In the birthplace of democracy, under a sky of luxuriant blue where olive groves leaned on hillsides and red fishing boats bobbed in coves, I worked and continued to ask the people I met as we wandered hotel grounds — out of earshot from colleagues and guests — "So what do you like about your job?" If the pause before answering was too long, I'd add, "Just between you and me, of course." And, the question that illuminated more: "What brought you here?"

Their name tags and uniforms varied but I plotted our common humanity. Our desire to improve; to help our family; to take the step our ambition knows is necessary; to find interesting people with whom to spend our time; to not like anything at all about our work but have an idea there's something better just around the corner.

But this niggled: *Does anybody really care what I'm doing? Tripping all over the place, sizing up hotels. What does it matter?*

I wasn't sure what The Englishman made of it either.

The Greek sunshine had no answer that May. But Tony and Maureen did. I found them by the pool at a tiny two-star property a few miles from the nearest town, on the Halkidiki Peninsula.

"Aye, what you doin' there?" asked a glistening bronzed man who could have been anywhere from 40 to 60.

"Oh, I'm just writing a review," I said, perched in a skirt on the edge of a sun lounge — a delicate balance I'd come to perfect.

"Ooooh, are you from Lonely Planet?" asked the lady lying next to the man, not giving me a chance to answer before turning to him, slapping his shoulder with the back of her hand and adding, "We might be famous, Tony!"

"No, I'm not from Lonely Planet," I said. That was my most-received question by then. "I write for *Gazetteers*, they're a travel guide for UK—"

"We know those ones, don't we, Maureen? Those books you get under the counter at the travel agent?"

"They're the ones!" No one had ever recognised the name before. "They're also known as 'the truth books'," I added, just to be sure we were talking about the same thing.

Tony and Maureen looked at each other and sat up to continue our conversation.

"We read them every time we go away," Tony said.

"He's only got a few weeks off each year — we want to make the most of it, not get ripped off by some fancy hotel brochure," chimed Maureen.

"So you find the reviews helpful then?" I asked, delight swelling at the prospect of truly helping all the Tonys and Maureens who had to make a little go a long way. For the Tonys and Maureens who, until that moment, had just been a figment in my head, implanted by a brief training trip to Benidorm seven months earlier where the details of our audience had been shared.

"Oh yes. That's how we decide. We look at all the write ups for all the places we're thinking of going. Haven't had one wrong yet," Tony said.

"You're really from the *Gazetteers*? Fancy that!" Maureen said.

I slept at my own two-star *pensione* more easily that night, my frustrations at its utilitarianism, gone. Purpose, it seemed, wasn't just for other people after all.

———

I sat on Bulgarian sand and looked out across the Black Sea, watching people parasailing. Their hoots of joy spread thin into the fine air on a sunny afternoon.

Soon after I'd arrived, the guy who looked like he was in charge had beckoned me over, towards the speedboat.

"Hey, do you want a ride?"

It was just a reflex to say no, wasn't it?

My internal assault had begun.

'No,' like you did to all the touts in the street (though one still managed to talk you into buying sunglasses at the twilight markets — who buys sunglasses when it's nearly dark?) and 'no,' to the taxi drivers hustling at the gate to the resort. There's only so much 'no' you can put into one life.

As the boat roared again, I concentrated on each new ascent, as if I were rising with each person into the cerulean, nothing mattering below.

There will be no proper reason you can give yourself when you look back on this about why you didn't try parasailing. None that makes sense or is true.

I wondered how rigorous the safety precautions were; how well the harness was attached.

My current book, Simon Winchester's *The Map that Changed the World,* sat neglected next to me, though I'd been devouring it. I'd brought it in the hope I could take time out on the beach and put work and everything else away for a while. I wanted to shake off weariness and the echo of the horrendous cover band in the hotel next door that had kept me awake for the previous six nights.

You've sat here for 30 minutes now, watching people go up and come down.

I rumbled with yearning to be up there too, to feel like I could fly, to press the idea of how I thought it would be, against the reality of being harnessed to a speedboat, scooting up, up above the holidaymakers — the Germans and the Italians outstripping the English; English relegated to third language on all the menus for the restaurants in town.

But inertia was swallowing me — a little creature caught by the water, mind whirring and humming — my desire for action too weak.

Get up! Don't, even for a second, think you can say you didn't go because you might have had a baby inside you.

The possible consequences were myriad. There was a lot to sift.

That nasty voice in my head was adept at making me feel stupid.

"Oh my god, will you shut up!" I said under my breath as I

shifted in the sand, the vocalisation an attempt to escape myself.

With 'friends' like you, who needs enemies? Just leave me alone.

*And regarding your comments the other day, **of course** I would like to know more about the history of the place I'm in. I can see Albena's Communist architecture and see the people embracing tourism and no, I don't know how they got here. I don't know the specifics of the regime and its downfall. I'm exploring, I'm finding these things in front of me that I don't understand and it makes me thirst for more, but there's only so much time. I can only deal with so much at one time too.*

I didn't want children; I never had. There was a look people got when I revealed that — an emotional cocktail from which I could only extract what I thought was pity at my own inability to know myself, and a dash of smugness. Most times followed by, "You might think that now, but you'll change your mind."

And you know what? If I am pregnant, it's a big fucking deal. So piss off. I'm doing the best I can.

My contract end was days away.

I'm working hard and I'm drinking a crap load of water trying to feel healthy and I don't know what I'm going to do for work next.

The speedboat's throttle dropped an octave and a woman in a pink bikini landed on the beach, cheering and fist-pumping the air.

So don't you dare give me a hard time for not going parasailing. I'm sitting on my own wondering if I'm not alone at all and if there is a life inside me. And does that change everything in ways I couldn't even conceive? God, what if he wants it?

Conceive! Ha!

I shook my head as I lay back on the sand and closed my eyes.

You wouldn't make a good mother, you know. You're a bitch. I'm quite nice — but I'd hate to unleash you on a child. It would never recover.

20

"Yeah, nothing says 'Relax, you're on holiday!' like two burly men with Kalashnikovs guarding the luggage carousel at the airport," I said.

"Really?" Naomi said as The Englishman poured her boyfriend more wine. "What was your hotel like?"

"Well, we landed in Bulgaria just before midnight and there was a bus ride through complete darkness — not a streetlight anywhere — for about 45 minutes, so I had no idea where we were going. It was weird to wake up in a Black Sea beach resort the next morning. Luckily my hotel was one of the ones that had been done up reasonably well, by local standards," I said.

"So what are you going to do next, Sara?" asked Naomi's boyfriend.

"The great job hunt continues!"

The four of us were sitting on the floor eating takeaway in a box-strewn, two-bedroom apartment in Sevenoaks — a leafy town just southeast of London, in Kent. The Englishman had re-joined the London 9–5, after the timber business in France had faltered, and we were yet to buy furniture. All we had was a bed. One of us had dug out the portable stereo, so we probably had

Nora Jones and Diana Krall playing in the background for our first impromptu 'dinner party'.

High summer twilight would peep through the elevated living room windows until about 10.30pm. Naomi and I took the empty food containers into the kitchen.

"I'm so glad you're here, honey — just down the road from us!" Naomi said.

We did our own little happy dance and hugged.

"You know what though?" I said.

Naomi leaned against the kitchen bench and raised an eyebrow.

"While I was away, I thought I was pregnant."

"What?! Are you? Hang on, 'thought'?"

"I sat on the beach for hours one day. Picked up a test from the pharmacy — charades and all to actually buy it! — and read the pamphlet to discover it's best done if you use your pee from first thing in the morning. So, of course, I didn't sleep much that night but—"

"But...?"

"I had my period when I woke up. After the relief, I was a bit annoyed I had to throw away a perfectly good test, so I did it anyway, just to be doubly sure."

"Oh, hon. Did you tell him?"

"Nope."

"Are you going to?"

"I'm not planning to."

We exhaled simultaneously and re-joined the boys.

———

"Hi, darling," it was The Englishman's voice on the phone, "I hope we haven't made a big mistake."

"Oh? Why do you say that?"

"I mean moving from Wandsworth to Sevenoaks. I've been in a traffic jam trying to get onto the A2 and I'd hate to drive this every night."

"Oh, what a pain. Perhaps there's just an accident. Let's hope so; well, I'm not hoping for an accident, you know what I mean."

"I know. You should have seen it earlier — we were all stopped and some man jumped out of his car and just took a piss at the side of the road. A load of others did the same, and I thought 'When in Rome...'!"

"When you've gotta go, you've gotta go, I guess! Well, I hope you're not stuck too long, sweetheart. There'll be some dinner here when you get home."

———

Throughout summer I delighted in our small, straggly back garden — once I'd pulled out all the nettles. Gloved and determined, I'd launched into the stinging, sweaty, tentative work with no idea just how tenacious those plants could be. With red feathery blotches still angry on my arms, I led The Englishman down the winding path to the back.

"Look at how much room there'll be here once all these are gone," I said, motioning across a half-cleared patch; earth showing where grass would hopefully then spread with the nettle scourge removed.

"Nice work!"

"Hey, I reckon we should put a table and chairs here."

The following weekend we constructed a little picnic table from a flat-pack kit from the hardware store. While we were at it, we splurged and grabbed a few citronella candles mounted in holders atop spiked cane rods.

"That'll keep those mosquitoes away!" I said, triumphant.

———

As autumn encroached, most nights after dinner, The Englishman went into the spare room to play computer games and I curled up in bed with a library book and listened to quiet jazz. For the first time in my life, I had matching bedside tables. That felt very grown up. Thanks to IKEA, they were topped with lamps shaped like ice cubes.

*Not **too** grown up.*

And the music soothed as I turned the pages and stories welled around me.

Then there were days when the wanderlust raged. The tedium and poor pay of my gift shop job were intolerable and the desire to move burned and bubbled within me. Every day was like a scratchy jumper I couldn't get off quickly enough, but I had to keep putting it on.

The Englishman wasn't enjoying his work either. He hadn't been accustomed to others' schedules for a while. He didn't like rules. Rules were for other people.

For the first time during the year we'd been together, I felt more bound than free.

I made bright pockets by catching the train 35 minutes up to London and having lunches or dinners with Charlotte and Naomi.

Samantha and I would occasionally meet near Waterloo or Charing Cross and find a 2-for-1 pizza lunch deal nearby, and we'd dream of other jobs and talk travel and relationships. Or I'd visit her studio apartment in Richmond — fabrics by Laura Ashley; scent by Jo Malone — while she whipped up a tasty stir fry.

Sometimes The Englishman and I ventured out on a Sunday together.

Aren't I too young to be doing the Sunday drive thing?

We criss-crossed Surrey and Kent and the tall-hedge-flanked country roads wended their own spell. The over-the-hill-and-far-away spirit came beckoning: *Keep going; keep driving. Monday morning is a trap. You could be halfway across Europe by then...*

There, with the world washing across the canvas of a windscreen, The Englishman and I fit so well.

––––––

The minutiae of daily monotony piled upon me in five months. The rut had become deep. The Englishman was there too but he dug at his own side of the trench.

I only have six months left in the UK. I can't spend it like this.

A middle-aged woman with perfect hair, nails and lashings of Botox basically threw Christmas cards onto the counter in front of me and looked out the gift shop window.

"Just these, madam?" I asked as I began ringing them up.

"Yes," she snapped.

She spent almost the equivalent of my weekly wage on greeting cards alone. I wondered if she had neck troubles from holding her nose so high all the time.

Later, I would grumble to Henry Hoover — a bright red machine with cartoon eyes and 'Henry' emblazoned in thick lettering on the side — as I vacuumed the closed store. I mumbled, "Five years of tertiary education to travel halfway around the world to earn just over five quid an hour. It doesn't seem right, does it, Henry?"

"Have you seen the shit I have to eat?" he'd reply.

Then I'd reconcile the day's takings on the till and walk 20 minutes' home in the near-snowing dark.

The only happy things about mid-winter were the prospects

of Christmas and potentially the beginning of another hotel-reviewing season.

Dear god, let them renew my contract.

21

I went to the bathroom for the third time. I'd only had a few hours' sleep and 4.30am in late January had come far too soon.

There is no way you're not getting on that plane. You've got a job to do. Come on, it's time to go. Get yourself together.

I hate this. It's like I'm at war with myself. I can't find the pattern to this nausea and stomach upset...it doesn't happen every time I travel. It's hit and miss. What is it? I want to go — I so deeply want to be out there again so what's the problem?

Just as I was picking up my bags to dash out to the waiting taxi, The Englishman kissed me in a way that broke me apart a little. I wanted nothing more than to stay wrapped up in our bed.

"Let me know," he said.

"I will as soon as I get back," I replied.

Discomfort at the edge of his voice: "That's not for a week."

"I have to run. I love you. 'Bye."

On a sunny winter afternoon, high in the French–Italian Alps, no one knew exactly where I was and I had no phone reception as I rounded a sharp bend and hit the brakes. I stared at the rockslide. Half the road in front of me had fallen away, who-knows-how-far down the side of the snow-drenched mountain. I couldn't go backwards, the corner was blind. I couldn't stay where I was. If I went forwards, it would be doing so without any idea of the stability of the remaining section of the (wrong side of the) road.

Time ballooned.

You got your adventure. You've been tripping around the world. You should have enjoyed it a bit more, eh? Maybe this is where it ends. It would be quite the high to go on, don't you think?

The part of my brain that usually entered into a dialogue said nothing.

Don't you think?

No reply.

After seconds or minutes: *It's so peaceful up here.*

The sunshine bathed me in silence. I could feel my lungs expanding; a reflex to savour the air stripped bare. Only climbers on the world's tallest mountains reached further into the cobalt sky than I did at that moment. Everything was beautiful.

After seconds or minutes: *Screw it.*

I held my breath, slammed down the accelerator and got as close to the mountain as I could, shimmying across the remaining section of road, easing the car so close to the rock face the wing mirror could have kissed it.

Maybe this is the moment to start believing in God...

There wasn't a second for looking anywhere other than straight ahead — to the smooth bitumen on the other side of the gash; beyond the rocks strewn at the edge of the earth wound.

And there was no sound and there was no time and there was no life flashing before my eyes. Just a riot of energy pillaging my body, pulling me and the car across the road, far, far above the valleys I'd peeked into just a few minutes earlier.

For a slow-motion instant I was more than I had ever been.

When I made it to the other side, I was James Bond.

———

The wooden pew was hard beneath my backside and though it was early February, I don't remember seeing my breath mist in the air. But it wasn't warm. The Alpine church was just a pocket of silence near the clouds; its interior restrained. Not like the gaudy flashings of the ornate churches I'd seen in some parts of Italy and Greece. Nor were there echoes of the Gothic intricacies found at cathedrals in Winchester or Canterbury.

I'd seen a few churches by then, comparing houses of God — whichever God — as I wandered. Making a catalogue of architecture and worship, always enthralled by the peace inside. Inside the buildings, and in *me* when I was in *them*.

This time, I let my gaze rest on the narrow stained-glass windows behind the simple elevated altar. I felt luminescent.

In a deep recess that had tucked away large and small fears in tight-knit bundles, there was one tremendous exorcism. A purging of doubt and a welling of contentment. Where the phosphorescence I'd seen at sea came out to play again and I was wired into the possibility and hope wrung through life.

I don't want to forget this moment. When everything was right; is right.

And I can't quite explain it but I'm going to keep it within me, for the future, if I need it. Because this is powerful. All is well. Everyone is okay. Mum and Dad, Nana and Pop, my brother. I have good friends.

I'm out in the wild again and soaking in the globe. And that precious man is waiting for my answer...I told him I felt like we were only just starting; that I didn't want to go...he didn't want me to go either.

But I want this in-between time; high in the Alps, in a tiny church, where I am alone with the magnificence of the world.

————

One February day near London I turned 26. It was 2004.

The Englishman and I looked in the jeweller's window in Sevenoaks high street and a narrow bevel-edged platinum band caught my eye. It fit perfectly. It made my long slim fingers look elegant. I pulled him close with my other hand.

I came all this way to find you.

After my birthday dinner in London with several friends, old and new, The Englishman and I stole away to Normandy for a few days, to the property near Savigny-le-Vieux.

We argued about something — I don't remember what — but afterwards I lay next to him in bed, quietly wounded and I whispered, "I hate conflict. I don't want to fight."

"Conflict is a natural part of a relationship. It *will* happen. If you can't get used to that, now is the time to say something," he said.

Seared, I reeled into all the arguments I'd ever witnessed and overheard. I couldn't think that he, that *we*, could occupy the same place. The place that was vicious and lonely; that I always tried to lock away.

And I was still trying to suppress it at 35,000 feet, on my way to my next assignment.

————

Ceiling fans stirred in the high white ceilings. Cool air eddied across the dark timber and black-and-white-checkered floors, licking my ankles. I left the rest of Jamaica outside. The quiet, unhurried order of Montego Bay's Round Hill was a sip of respite. It was neat and inviting and 'lived in' all at once.

I laid back for a moment into the cushioned lounge chair and let my gaze drift outside to the thriving greenery and placid ocean. A view topped by a navy-blue-and-white-striped awning. I slowed my breath and let the faint scent of frangipani and sea air fill me; I pushed my shoulders down, undoing their hunch.

Above the reception area and the bar were a host of framed black and white photos — white matt, black frame — of many people of note who'd visited the hotel since its opening in the early 1950s. JFK had honeymooned there with Jacqueline. Other distinguished guests included a few European socialites, American stage and film stars and various politicians.

Noel Coward was one of the first shareholders. Ian Fleming spent time living and writing in Jamaica too. I imagined the two of them roaring up what must have been a dirt track, to the place in which I sat, for a liquid evening carousing around the piano with all the other British ex-pats who'd escaped post-war England.

How I'd love to have been at one of those nights.

I needed a few sentences about the grounds, so I followed a little trail down the hill to a beach in a cove. It was perfect. Just as I hoped the day would be in three weeks' time.

———

At home in the quiet of an early morning in spring, with only a few birds roused, I perched on the end of the bed on my own. I paused a moment before opening what I held in my lap;

admiring the small satin flowers and ribbons Mum had carefully woven through the holes punched at the side of the few pages of paper. Tracing my finger across the embellished script on the title page, I felt the heart: 'For Sara, on her Wedding Day'.

If I'd cried after I'd read Mum's poem, my make-up would have run and it was the first time I'd used liquid eyeliner so I looked up and sniffed and blinked instead.

The wish that she and Dad could have been there was one that I couldn't let in. Thankfully it was quickly quelled by my anticipation, full-bodied and dreamy. Like Christmas morning as a kid, in the hours before the presents can be opened. I carefully tucked the poem away and whispered, "Thank you, Ma. Dad, you know I love you too."

I woke Charlotte and Naomi from their deep sleep in the spare room. My hen's night dinner had been a little rougher on them.

"Oh my god, Sara, you're already dressed," Charlotte said, "and you've done your make up too! You look gorgeous."

"Honey, you look beautiful," Naomi said.

I did a little twirl on tip toes, burgundy satin falling nearly to the floor.

"Thank you."

The Englishman drove the four of us to a stately old building. Naomi took artful and candid photos. Charlotte tried not to cry. I got the giggles during the ceremony and The Englishman knew it was just nerves. He squeezed my hand.

Afterwards, we all drank champagne.

Later, my husband and I had a candle-lit dinner in the West Country, tucked in a corner of the city of Bath; its Georgian architecture, handsome sandstone and postcard countryside, ignored for a little while.

When The Englishman smiled as we woke on our

honeymoon the next morning, life had never been as exquisite as in that moment.

I didn't yet know how I was indebted to my mother-in-law for that long weekend of bliss.

22

Rome, your elegant chaos was seductive. You were an old soul in Prada, Gucci — pick a costume. The seat of an empire, faded.

My inner imp revelled in one of your hotels: a heaven and hell theme, triumphant. Just sitting in the lobby made me feel the spark of all things sensual was painted onto the walls and stitched into the fabric of the lounges. Converted from an old bank, the property's sandstone facade belied a very different experience than the one it projected onto the street. Conversing with the Italian staff left me happily aquiver; review, complete.

But that was an exception.

Mostly I walked you with memories of how The Englishman and I had found you on our runaway trip 15 months earlier. Your history and mine, entwined. You, with the trump card of grandeur and millennia, your wanting and mine, entwined.

The Englishman felt more than a couple of countries away.

I tried to concentrate on my current itinerary that zig-zagged me across you, Rome. Until, whether I concentrated or not, it was time to go north.

———

Siena buoyed me briefly. The glow of the stone walls in the old city was as alluring as the poets and historians and guidebooks suggested. There were potted plants with red blooms mounted on green window shutters. Young and old couples ambled. The air was delicate — its knotted winter heaviness gone.

My cosy room with a view was welcome too. Framed in the pre-sunset 'golden hour', it was all Tuscan stone farm houses peeping from groves of greenery. All undulating hills, cross-hatched with ploughed fields and white-blossom-laden trees. Low ash-blue mountains rimmed the scene. I knew I'd yearn for that room and its window in the future.

This is the perfect place to write a book...

Though there was no undoing the abruptness with which I'd crashed after the honeymoon.

It was hard to be grateful and horrified at the same time. My mother-in-law had sworn the family to secrecy for three days: my father-in-law had almost severed his hand in an accident at work on the day we'd married. And no one ever said it, but I couldn't kill the concern that all The Englishman's family were thinking, 'This wouldn't have happened if we'd been invited to your wedding.'

The Englishman trekked between England and France again, working long hours in the revived timber business on behalf of his recuperating father. A week into married life and our communication was text messages and missed calls and calling cards all over again.

Everything and nothing was the same.

My mood was black and unshakeable by the time I got to Florence. I trudged in the rain looking for somewhere to eat. The city was a pressing aural amplification: brittle horns, tramping feet, the snap of umbrellas. The cold and the foreignness of it all became corrosive.

When my aimless restaurant search took me past the *Duomo*, I was empty.

Yes, it's a 13th-century cathedral with one of the only remaining examples of green marble...blah blah...whatever. Have you got any decent food, Florence?

Wet and miserable, I ate oily, tasteless lasagna in a tourist trap.

You're in Florence! You've become just like those ship passengers who couldn't even smile at the prospect of a cruise.

Yeah, well, maybe they had stuff going on; I shouldn't have judged them...

The rain seeped into my dreams as I fell asleep that night in a four-poster bed in a sumptuous room with a view to the Arno River, just beyond the Ponte Vecchio. And I appreciated none of it.

Until the sun bathed the city two mornings later and it was a Renaissance painting blooming with light and texture. Looking from my window to the opposite side of the river, I could see the thin buildings in muted yellow, terracotta and cream, all sandwiched together but standing tall; proud, almost iridescent.

Grabbing my camera, I ran outside without breakfast, snapping all I could in the 45 minutes before I had to leave for the airport.

I raced past the merchants and artisans on the Ponte Vecchio. I swooned at the perfection of florists' displays framed by arches; at cobbled alleyways climbing towards the river and disappearing around corners. Even the simplicity of a nun walking past a bright yellow wall brought a smile behind my lens.

The most decadent discovery on that whiplash photo tour?

The little bustling pocket of a place that sold hot chocolate —
liquid chocolate, with a dash of milk.

Italy! **Now** *you woo me. Just as I have to go... Sorry, but there's*
someone waiting for me. I need to go home to my husband. 'My
husband'. I love saying that!

———

I got the call in The Netherlands, about 10 days after I'd left Italy.
As I was leaning against a long rack of bicycles outside
Amsterdam Central Station, arranging hotel questionnaires in
my laptop bag, my husband's name came up on the tiny black
and white screen of my phone.

"Would you like to live in France for a while and renovate
that house?"

"Yes."

Without missing a beat. Yes. With love. Yes. With all I
had. Yes.

"We could go in summer. Once you've finished this contract;
after your mum's come to visit?"

"Let's do it!"

———

Mum had previously been overseas 30 years earlier, in 1974.
She'd announced only weeks after she and Dad had met that
she was accompanying him on his posting to London. They set
up house in Kent for a year and lived in sin. Mum was a legal
secretary; Dad still got paid in Australian dollars, one of which
bought three British Pounds at the time. The sin had been
comfortable.

Her eyes shone in the living room in Sevenoaks when she

told The Englishman and me about her first glimpse of Edinburgh Castle a few weeks earlier.

"You know, it was just awe-inspiring. Oh, I walked for hours! Along the Royal Mile; I *had* to sample the shortbread, and I *may* have been into the cashmere store…"

"Did you get your ear in to the accents okay?"

"Yes, but not that I needed to — there were Australians everywhere! Sara, you'd have been proud, I found my way back to the hotel without a drama. Easy peasy," Mum said, straightening, with a little nod and a tap of her palm on her knee; Dad's criticism about her lack of direction, refutable.

Her mum had always wanted to see Scotland, and Mum's sadness it had never happened tempered her enthusiasm a little. But as her tales about the lochs and the Highlands unravelled over dinner, it was clear to all of us Mum's appetite for the world was a bright and splendid thing.

"So you didn't talk Dad around at the last minute then?" I smiled wryly.

She shook her head. We changed the subject.

When she and I were in the kitchen, my voice low but eyebrows raised: "So, what do you think?"

I hope you like my husband.

"Apart from him not wearing a seatbelt on the M25 when we were driving back from Heathrow…"

"Yeah, I know. I hate that too; I've spoken to him about it—"

"He makes you laugh a lot. It's nice to watch you together," she smiled.

"I can't wait for you to come and visit us in Normandy."

23

Normandy. In high summertime light, we feasted; you were bountiful in bloom. A kingdom. I skirted your cross-hatched fields in my little old black car, right-hand drive on the right, staring down the roadside ditches. You were long days and hope and window boxes and bubbling French — thick-cut with the North, I was told — old. Language as old as your ruins.

A tractor hummed in the distance somewhere; a French farmer working the evening light. A singular sound against our gaggle of about eight. Half my new family — and their friends. We'd all tumbled into a villa for a week or so while making our cottage about 50 kilometres (30 miles) up the road habitable.

We thwacked golf balls across the valley, popped air rifles, poured wine and set the long wooden table in the old kitchen for a mini feast. A feast that was really a simple dinner, but hard work had made us all hungry. Cutlery and glass clunked, bread was buttered and the dance of the serving bowls began.

I elbowed my way into the great tousle of the four brothers' conversation and sought side-long smiles from the few at the table who, by long association but unbound by genetic ties, had perfected stepping in and out of the madness unscathed.

Home wasn't half a world away anymore. The Englishman's brothers would return to the UK soon and the two of us would stay.

Later that evening, in the golden last light, he kissed me as we stood on the front steps of that borrowed villa and said, "I'm the happiest I've ever been."

———

On a few weekends, The Englishman and I allowed ourselves to explore nearby.

Villages and woods near St Fraimbault were luxuriant with flowers. Blooms tumbled from hanging pots on wrought iron street lanterns and window boxes, and they weighed down cottage gardens. They flaunted their colour in the wild on sun-dappled roadsides. A riot of pink, red, white, gold, lilac and orange. Dahlias, delphiniums, marigolds and roses.

Polished clear skies were a gift and we ate when we pleased and I photographed the foreign world around me. I admired the stone and half-timbered houses, so distinct and unchanged through the previous centuries.

My jaw hung slack when I first saw the chateau at Bagnoles de l'Orne and we stole kisses in the car before we left the property's majesty.

———

"I just heard back from the editor of that magazine I told you

about. He wants 1200 words — *and* pictures — back in London
in 48 hours!" I gushed after hanging up the phone.

"Well, you'd better get started then," The Englishman said.

Thirty-six hours later, awash with deadline-induced fervour,
I sat on the floor and read my piece for submission aloud to The
Englishman while he was in the bath:

On a business trip to Amsterdam this year, my life
was changed forever. It's the sort of city where
anything can, and does, happen. The pivotal
moment came when my mobile phone rang. The
voice was my husband's: "Would you like to live in
France for a while and renovate that house?"

I said: "Yes."

I first saw the house in question two years ago,
when it was little beyond a ruin. It was neatly
tucked away at the end of a narrow lane, some
distance behind a farmhouse. Autumn had not yet
encroached on the surrounding fields and it was
delightfully peaceful. The man showing it to me
was an attractive Englishman I had just met. He'd
owned the property for a little while, but had no
specific plans for it. As he spoke, I silently took in
the fresh air — worlds away from London — and
pondered the probability that the first sounds of
the day here were likely to come from birds, not
motorcars. There were no clues I was looking at
my future home and husband on that sunny
afternoon in Normandy.

I returned to London from Amsterdam excited
by the challenge ahead. Relocating didn't bother
me — I had already come around the world from

Australia, so what harm could befall me going across the Channel? The language barrier would be tricky, but my new husband promised to teach me phrases from his fluent vocabulary. Ultimately the move made sense: my writing and photography work is transportable, and his timber flooring company requires he spend a lot of time in France anyway. I had only a minor sense of apprehension about my undertaking such a renovation — he was experienced with these projects, but my knowledge would have to increase exponentially. At least with a starting point of zero, the only place to go was up.

From the outset we planned to do most of the work ourselves. We were essentially working with the remnants of a 300-year-old oak-framed cottage that had been renovated and extended with breeze-block in ensuing years, prior to his purchase. Though it had been half timbered at one stage, there were few timbers remaining. Only half the building was roofed, and the interior was in a poor state of repair. The whole place was damp from years of exposure, the garden was wild and littered with building debris, but there was promise in our little house, near the Norman town of Domfront.

The intended timeframe of the rebuild/renovation is one year, and two-and-a-half months into the project, that still seems realistic. Making the place habitable has been the first priority and thankfully we are almost at the end of that stage, despite some interesting events along the way. Rotting, ancient timbers of the half-

roofed section have been removed, and a local
roofer assisted us with a new construction.
Completing the roof gave us a remarkable
psychological boost, and it was with renewed
focus we turned our attention to item two: the
septic tank.

Most people would not associate the
installation of a septic tank with a near-death
experience, but it depends on who is operating the
backhoe. My husband and his family have lived in
France intermittently for more than a decade, and
during this time they've made numerous eccentric
local friends. One, nicknamed 'The Professor', is a
characterful retired gentleman with a gift for
fixing anything mechanical. He has crazy white
hair, a zest for life (and the ladies) and also
operated backhoes during his working life: the
perfect man for the septic tank job? Maybe.

I had been out at the supermarket for the
morning, practising my smattering of French on
checkout operators and trying to increase my
vocabulary by memorising various food names
(you have to start somewhere). I arrived onsite
with fresh croissants, baguettes and pâté for my
husband and father-in-law, but it quickly became
clear they weren't in the mood to eat. The
Professor had been reacquainting himself with the
backhoe controls: the corner of the (new) roof was
now rubble on the ground, and in another deft
manoeuvre, half of the ancient well in the front
garden had been demolished. Then as the
Professor was removing a pile of debris near
where my husband was working, he hit the wrong

lever. The hulking metal arm of the machine quickly swung around 90 degrees, at head height. Lucky he has fast reflexes!

And it's also fortunate he has four brothers. We managed to convince three of them and a friend to come and help us with the house for a few weeks in the summer, so the property progressed dramatically as strapping lads with building know-how set to work on making the interior of the original house habitable. In quieter moments, when the drills, saws, hammers and generator had stopped, I remembered with a smile my initial contemplation of the morning birdsong and the peace and quiet. Having friends and family over was a great bonus work-wise, and it also gave us the chance to explore the region during time off.

D-Day beaches, the cities of Caen and Rouen, and the fairytale abbey of Mont-Saint-Michel, all cater to different tastes, but a favourite of mine is a packed picnic and a drive to watch the world go by. Because Normandy is primarily an agricultural region, the landscape changes dramatically with the seasons. Crops are sown and harvested, wildflowers blanket the fields and hedges, then slowly retreat, and there is a harsh beauty to the starkness of it all in winter, especially when it snows. But the farmers are out working whatever the weather, and their primary mode of transport is the tractor. As I soon discovered that just as Londoners plan a journey anticipating Tube delays, the equivalent rule in France is the 'tractor factor'. When driving the tiny lanes — with plentiful blind corners — it is possible to end up behind a tractor for some time, so relax and enjoy the scenery on these occasions.

Inevitably friends and family went home and it was just the two of us back on the tools. We recently celebrated two momentous events at the house: first came the connection of the water, and then the electricity. Soon we will actually be able to move in! The past months have involved hauling possessions from one spare room to another, on the invitation of kind friends and family, but the next time we move it will be into our very own construction site. And then I really must put a serious effort into learning French.

We were visiting the Professor and his wife recently (who don't speak any English) and I was obliviously nodding and smiling along to the French conversation. Then I heard a few words which I thought I understood, and judging by the Professor's hand movements assumed he was reliving the drama of the septic tank installation. At this point everyone suddenly looked at me. "What are they saying?"

"The Professor just asked if we were going to have a baby next year."

I laughed and laughed; it seems even the sign language is different here.

The Englishman was still. My voice, a little hoarse. My heart, its own flurry of electricity.

"Nicely done," he said.

Quatre timbre pour Australie, s'il vous plaît.

I was in the post office, nervously flipping the phrase over and over in head, hoping I could eject it perfectly just as I got to the little window. Four stamps for Australia, please.

Quatre timbre pour Australie, s'il vous plaît.

My default second language was Japanese. My brain smashed together unintelligible hybrid sentences — half French and one quarter English and one quarter Japanese. So I cherished tiny triumphs at the post office or *boulangerie* or market.

Amid that linguistic bloodshed, I decided 'Wednesday' was my favourite French word: *Mercredi*. Not much to look at but lovely to say. It was fulsome in my mouth, like some large round sweet that was too hard to chew but too big to swallow, my tongue rolling around it.

I discovered years later that synaesthesia is responsible for the phenomenon of interchanging sensory input; an example is attaching colours to numbers, letters and words. So for me, in English 'Wednesday' was royal blue. In French, I could taste it. Wednesday became like caramel.

But French never really loved me and I never practised enough. I don't know if it would have made a difference to anything that was to come.

24

"Our recent audience survey has shown the average age of a Radio 4 listener is 54," the BBC announcer said. "We'll be reporting more on the results shortly but for now, sit back, relax, it's time for the Afternoon Play."

I stopped sanding the skirting board in the bathroom.

Oh my god. I'm 26 and the highlight of my day is the Afternoon Play.

I made myself a cup of tea and sat on the front step in the sun. Looking over the field rimmed by trees with autumn leaves, in my dirty clothes and paint-spattered boots, I blew on my steaming brew and waited for the play to start.

This is sad. People would kill for this chance to renovate a cottage in the middle of France and you're most excited by BBC radio. It's a top day if you can catch a re-run of Neighbours on BBC2 later in the afternoon, eh?

But I like the radio because it keeps me company and attached to the world.

Is this what old people who live alone feel like all the time?

While the Afternoon Play theme song trilled, I realised how

comfortable I was in scuffed and faded garments — clothes for dirty work. Adam and I always had jobs to do on the farm after school so we'd forever be throwing our uniforms into the wash on our way back outside in work clothes.

Adam. I thought of him briefly, living near Mum and Dad, his work split between days and nights in pubs and restaurants, splicing in life where he could. He and I had drifted, and I missed our childhood selves, but Mum tied our orbits together — she was the satellite relay.

I wiped wood dust off my pants. Those work clothes meant, in more than any other way I'd found, that I could point to a thing at the end of my day and say, "I did that." My efforts were tangible and part of something bigger I was creating with someone else — with the man who had me at "Hello".

———

One Sunday morning I was lying on my side on the hard floor of the small room that was our kitchen and living area all-in-one. I was scraping old paint off the wall or putting new paint on it. Whatever the task, it was awkward and uncomfortable and I'd been doing it for a while when the church bells rang.

The exultant melody pealed across the fields. I stopped to listen and felt an involuntary smile.

Oh, it's a wedding! I wish you well. It may not be what you think, the path ahead, but today the world is yours.

I pictured the significant day for people I'd never met in the tiny church nearby I'd never visited. And I hoped they'd be happy because 'happy' was proving harder than I'd thought.

———

"That delivery is ready to go to England so we'll need to be on the ferry for the early crossing tomorrow morning to get it to London in time," The Englishman said, taking his boots off. "That means we'll have to be up about 3.15."

"Oh. I'm thinking about staying here," I said.

"What? You're not coming?"

"Well, you always said I didn't have to come, that it was up to me. You see, I've started writing a short story; these characters have just come out of nowhere and—"

"You're just going to stay here *and write*?"

"Yeah. I haven't written anything for *ages* and it actually feels really exciting. You look angry. What's the problem?"

He barely said a word before he left. I wrote through the day and into the following night; I found the way back into my own imagination and the characters it made felt so real. The release was palpable.

"Hey, welcome home! I didn't hear from you, did everything go okay?" I asked.

"It was fine," he said.

"I really got into the characters with my writing; it was so much fun. It's been too long since I've done anything creative. Do you want to read my story?"

"No."

———

We'd argued again. I don't remember now what all the fighting was about, but it tangled us in ever-constricting knots, barbed with hurt and doubt.

I sought solace in the hot shower. Tears ran in rivulets down my face, shampoo suds down my back. The wedge-shaped shower stall was too small in the tiny bathroom in the big world — and nothing was washing away the heartache that had begun far too soon.

Stepping out onto the bath mat, I didn't even try to silence my sobs, coming in gulping waves. He heard me and came into the bathroom, wrapped his arms around the towel that was wrapped around my shoulders and I buried into his dark woollen jumper. How I needed that solace. My skinny white still-dripping legs couldn't fully hold me in that moment.

"Hey," he said, pushing my wet hair from my cheeks as I sniffed and wiped one eye with my hand, "we meant our vows, didn't we?"

"Yes! Yes, we did."

"Because I'm at the point where we can sweep all this under the carpet, you know? Rewind; start again."

How I wanted to start again.

I wanted to go back to our busy, shining, hopeful time. To the mornings of possibility and the evenings that welled with satisfaction. To the work that made our little house come together — "Look, darling, I've painted the wall!" — to our day-trip jaunts when Normandy became less isolating, when he told me secrets and histories of that battle-worn swathe of country; when I admired his slip between English and French.

How I deeply wanted to reclaim the time we'd talk lightly about the day over dinner, drink wine and start again tomorrow. When a trip back across the Channel to England was a mini adventure. When I still felt strong and the loneliness hadn't begun to seep in, laying a pall over everything. When we didn't fight half the time.

I craved it all.

And I desperately wanted to be rid of the strange red rash that had started to flare on my cheek. Had I lived in the days of witch drowning, I would have been a marked woman.

———

The two of us went to Hertfordshire, England. To a grand manor house and spa, just outside the town of Tring.

We were tentative at breakfast. We weren't sure what was customary when eating an alarmingly healthy meal, dressed only in bath robes, in a plush room with a handful of strangers dressed in bath robes.

Are they all naked underneath?

"Just don't think about it," The Englishman said, reading my mind.

I luxuriated in a massage. My back and shoulders were a warren of knots. He gave me his 'free' massage appointment — opting to read in our well-appointed room in one wing of the manor house instead. I hadn't had a massage for years; I didn't know what I'd do with two in one day so I converted it to a manicure. I'd never had one of those.

We lazed together reading for a little while in the afternoon, yet to dress beyond fluffy white gowns and spa slippers.

"It's incredible how quickly we got used to living in our building site at home — this room just feels *so* decadent," I said. "It was a great idea to come here for a couple of days; thank you."

25

The whole of Normandy turned to mud in winter. Black trees scratched at bare-bones sky and I was hollow. As the fog and mud spread, somehow it conspired to compress: earth, air, breath.

The Englishman was still often away from the house, working long hours with his dad. He had conversations with French employees at night — in person, on the phone. Unintelligible drama. Knotted brows and hands thrown in the air. Dirty boot prints on the floor.

After a summer and early autumn of hard work on the house — cleaning, sanding, scraping, painting, insulating, tiling, installing — it all stopped. No more building supplies were purchased. The conjuring of a little home from a mammoth renovation must have become a feat too far.

But he never confided that. My questions were deflected. I didn't push. I couldn't handle another row.

One day I climbed up into the pitched roof space that had been insulated with the last of the supplies and converted into two small rooms and a landing. The rectangle of sky visible through the window in the roof was the colour of dark slate. I was painting the walls white with the remains of the paint bucket, and I started to sing.

Before I realised what I was doing, I'd put the paintbrush aside and I was pouring my soul into the mournful but rousing *I Dreamed a Dream*, looking skywards with a faltering voice. My unspoken worries and fears whirled, gathering and glowering from the corners of my mind. My throat constricted as I came to the final line of the song and I couldn't even bring myself to whisper it.

I was standing on an island in the dark, holding a lantern aloft, wondering where the man I loved had gone. I had no idea how to get back to him.

One evening he said, "I thought we'd get closer when we got married."

It seemed we were both sad.

I'm right here but you can't see me.

Then it began to snow.

————

The Englishman drove me to a tiny rural station and I waited on the platform, alone on a December afternoon, for a train to Paris. Even in that small step away, we missed each other.

 Shouldn't have left you at the station. I'm back at the house now and it's empty without you. Xx

I flew solo to Australia and surprised Mum for Christmas. Dad was my co-conspirator, and Naomi picked me up at the airport. I needed all their arms and the sun. Mum cried happy tears. My mother-in-law thoughtfully sent me 'a little something to open in the sunshine' while I was a hemisphere away from their celebrations.

When I returned, renewed, to Normandy, The Englishman and I shared 'I love you' in the murky mid-January daylight when we held each other, and I was sure we'd find our way home.

————

Weeks later, The Englishman fled one night after an argument, wheels spinning, roaring up our uneven drive. His second-hand dark green convertible dog-legged past the old lady's house at the top of the laneway and cut by pastures in the near-absolute winter darkness. I must have crumpled into sleep then — in *la maison dans le champ*; the house in the field — as the fire died and our three tiny rooms grew cold.

Gravel-crunch footsteps outside the cottage window after midnight should have alarmed me. But I was slow to wake. Adrenaline roared when I met the footsteps at the front door and saw a shaken, bloody, dirty face. My husband's: The Englishman's face.

"I crashed the car," he said. "I had to walk back."

When I'm generous, I remember rapid-firing the expected, "Are you all right? Are you sure? Was anyone else hurt? What happened? How far did you just walk?" Then, satisfied, slipping into shock-induced practicality.

When I'm brutal, I remember asking all those things. Then part of my brain walled in fury, futility and the urge to care and protect. An instant in which I subconsciously removed what I'd longed for from him: love in the face of hurt and fear.

"Take off all your clothes. Carefully. You've probably got glass all over you," I said.

I didn't want glass on the lounge, even though it was a cheap

IKEA futon with a throw over it. Nor stuck in the reclaimed timber flooring he'd installed, sanded and varnished several months earlier. Nor did I want shards 'lost' in the fleck of the bathroom tiles — the tiles that seemed to render everything invisible except the cream-coloured spots that dripped onto them from the door I'd painted.

Gingerly, he undressed. Everything corralled into a laundry basket: the enduring waterproof olive jacket, the navy-blue knitted jumper, perhaps underneath, a Stone Roses T-shirt. Jeans.

He showered.

I disinfected the minor wound near his brow, checked scrapes and asked if he felt dizzy, adding that we needed to watch for signs of concussion. He said he didn't need a doctor.

In bed, I stared at the ceiling. I wasn't just in a foreign country, another hemisphere, anymore. I'd strayed — *we* had strayed — into badlands. Neither of us knew how to get out alive. I asked the middle distance between our duck-down quilt and the moon:

"Do you want me to hug you?"

So hushed: "Yes."

In the morning, he assured me nothing was broken.

I drove us to the crash site, beyond a narrow back road seemingly miles away.

His car had flipped at least once after careening beyond a bend. Any passenger would have been flattened beneath, or into, buckled metal. Somehow there was an untouched 'bubble' just large enough for a driver with long legs. Just large enough for a driver who shouldn't have been on the road.

Everything had broken that night. It was just easier to tow away a car.

I was almost 27.

I'd half-packed my possessions. I don't remember if the packing began before or after the crash, but during February the boxes had become makeshift tabletops, sitting in the corner of the lounge area; their remaining capacity was the barometer of my marriage.

Mum emailed.

 Darling, should I post your wedding anniversary card? To *la maison dans le champ?* (It's from Dad too, of course.)

– Yes, Ma, please do. We had a long talk the other night. We really do love each other and we're going to work through this. It's been so good to talk to you and Dad lately, thank you for everything. I'm okay. We'll be fine. Looking forward to your card. Truck loads o' love, xox

I had meant every word.
But some things become untrue long before we ever know it.

Early March was still grey-pressed and cold in Northern France. There was no need for me to smuggle all the cold goods from the back of the car into the fridge as soon as possible. My instinct, born and hardened through so many Australian summers, was difficult to kill though. The groceries had survived another 40-minute drive, a few more minutes wouldn't hurt. Hell, frozen stuff even made it across the Channel when we stocked up in England and brought familiar brands and packages back to the chest freezer in the timber workshop.

Alone for the day, I turned the motor off outside our not-yet-half-renovated cottage and stared hard into the rear vision mirror for the longest time.

I remembered sitting at Mum and Dad's, almost three years earlier, leaning against my bedroom wall before I boarded the plane from Brisbane to Los Angeles to New York to London. *This is the decision point...there's all that's been...and all that happens after this...*

I looked at myself in that rear vision mirror as though it had the power to strip everything to its heart.

How did I get here?

*Is this relationship likely to change? Do you **know** how to make it better? Does he?*

What has to happen for it to be 'bad enough' to leave? Where's the line?

And since when did 'not that bad' become good enough?

Days later, I made a phone call.

———

"I'd like to book a flight from London Heathrow to Brisbane, Australia, please. One way," I said into the phone, several weeks after the crash.

There was no relief from the anguish when I hung up. The act of purchase was not the anaesthetic I wanted.

"What did you do today?" The Englishman asked as he came inside.

"I packed some more boxes," I said. "I booked my plane ticket."

"I'll have to book the ferry tickets."

During the next few days, I finished carefully packing and

labelling; filled out an inventory and all the paperwork for international transit, trying not to tear-blot the ink. The Englishman had agreed he would take it all to the London Heathrow depot of the shipping company, after letting me out at the airport's departures.

That was the plan. That's what he said he would do.

The Englishman had joked from the day we moved in together: "This won't all fit in a backpack anymore!" gesticulating grandly around any room we were in, in a parody of a waiter from our first night on our trip to Italy.

I'd always laugh: "Lucky it doesn't have to. I'm not going anywhere!"

––––––

My suitcase to check in was full to zip-strain bulge in the back of his white van. There were timber panels for delivery in there too, along with my boxes. Treasures, old and new.

We talked as though we were on any other trip. Until we didn't.

A three-hour drive from our cottage to Le Havre, a five-hour crossing of the English Channel to Portsmouth, at least a two-hour drive to London.

How can you just let me go? I don't want this to be real. I want you to ask me to stay. You're my husband. Please say something...?

26

L ondon. You were a heaving, seething, hulking city shot through with the sublime. Human confusions and ecstasies were writ large in you. Spite was buried in the stones of your Roman roads and desires drowned in the River Fleet. You were fractious and beautiful; stately and slovenly. Opportunity rippled throughout you like a slipstream.

I'd felt your possibilities on afternoons in Putney, sometimes at Sainsbury's and once near the crepe van by Westminster Bridge. I'd imagined the arcs of chance in the tunnels of the Tube, eddying as I ran for the train. I wanted to be intimate, London, but you had made so many masks and histories, I couldn't get as close as I wanted.

You were the city that sometimes burned and I wanted you to amplify my life.

In wishing so, I never thought I'd leave. I already had exit wounds from Heathrow, Gatwick and Luton Airports: Austria, Belgium, Bulgaria, Canada, Greece, Ireland, Italy, Jamaica, Spain, USA; part of the catalogue of my geographic infidelities. I couldn't stop. Those other places pushed themselves into my skin — splashing vistas and hollowing into my nose with their crisp and heady scents. Some had my attention for all the wrong reasons.

But I always came back to you, London, with the ghosts of foreign footsteps stuck to my shoes.

Normandy was always supposed to be temporary, too. We were coming back, he and I.

I knew you'd never noticed as I walked you again — through your grand thoroughfares and crooked alleys. When I peered into the Thames at dusk, I felt there was nothing I could keep from you that would ever match your secrets.

At St Paul's Cathedral for the first time, in my last hours with you, London, I told myself I was just a tourist and you were just a stopover.

Because I couldn't lose you and him at the same time.

———

Charlotte was back in Canada and I don't recall why I didn't see Samantha. But sweet Melissa — Charlotte's best friend whom I'd come to know — and her boyfriend, James, had tea, sympathy and a couch for my last night in the UK.

About a month earlier when I'd come to London to visit, Mel had hugged me as I stood and cried amid the lunchtime shoppers on Oxford St. My world was coming down. She'd wanted to make it better and we both knew she couldn't but I was unspeakably grateful she tried.

The Englishman stayed with a friend overnight. He picked me up from Mel and James' place to take me to the airport.

The true numbness hit at the departure terminal at Heathrow.

At the moment of our brief embrace and short kiss goodbye, I couldn't decide if the air between us was full of everything that wasn't spoken, or empty of anything to say.

I lost myself in the sea of passengers and found the appropriate queue to join so I could check in.

About two hours later the blankness was abating. I pulled another tissue from my handbag and blew my nose. In WHSmith I tried to square my shoulders against the foetal temptation.

Thirty minutes after that, at the boarding gate, I called him, thinking I was about to be sick. Thinking he might be somewhere nearby.

"Hi. It's me. Where are you?"

"I'm—I'm already back in Portsmouth." His faltering voice and a sniff in that one sentence was the first evidence of his upset.

"You just drove straight back?"

"Yes, well, what else was I going to do? You're about to get on a plane."

"But that's the thing, I don't want to — I don't want this. I want to stay."

"What about next time?"

"What do you mean?"

"What happens the next time we argue and we just end up in the same place?"

"I don't know. That's the point — I don't want there to be a next time."

"Just…Just go and see your mum for a while."

The world fell away below. I could only deal with five minutes at a time.

I read a little of my airport purchase when I could: Bill Bryson's *Neither Here, Nor There*; the dark irony needled me through dusk then a dawn on the other side of the planet.

———

Changi was a hellish halfway point. There was little respite for me in Singapore's gleaming international airport. I sat on the carpet, away from people but near the gate for my next flight. Clutching my passport that was barely a year old — the one with my maiden name had many more stamps — and the cover started to slick with perspiration. I tried to escape into the time between my shallow breaths.

I was 27. It was March 2005.

What if I just grabbed a last-minute ticket, turned around and flew back to London?

SIN to LHR was open a few gates away.

My body was inert. The tiny part of me that wasn't just staring at the floor remembered my visit to Singapore three years before: I'd docked at the port, gone window shopping on Orchard Road and laughed with Nick over lunch. He'd been merciless about my inability to use chopsticks. "The three year old on the table behind us is better than you!"

Nothing adhered to me from that spotless corner of airport carpet as I stood, but I habitually wiped off my clothes and straightened them anyway. My hands had a tremor no one could see as I sipped from my water bottle. My mouth stayed dry despite the drink. I shuddered and a fissure of panic opened within me.

Two flights were about to board. One to the UK. One to Brisbane, Australia. I joined a queue and tried not to think about what was happening.

I don't know how to do this.

PART IV

COMPASS | 2005–2009

AGE: 27–31

27

Australia, six months later

Brisbane, with your heat like a heavy coat. Even in springtime. With your clutch of shiny skyscrapers and colonial sandstone — set to a grid on one bend of your broad river; the wearers of suits swarming there, as though it were cooler.

You were not a raft of suburbs paved atop the hills and flats; no. You were a sprawling, big old town living *amongst* the palms, paperbarks, grevilleas and jacarandas. Amongst the creepers and orb-weaving spiders.

I admired your timber and tin houses — original and newly-plush: Queenslanders lived in 'Queenslanders'. Those places pushed up through the vegetation, living areas perched high on second floors; ground level traditionally left for little other than floodwaters and earth that was last dug between world wars.

The next wave of 'gentrification' was yet to sculpt you.

I could feel you breathe, Brisbane. Because like me, sometimes you didn't.

We were both waiting.

————

Let's hope she hasn't died, moved or changed her phone number.

'You're welcome back any time,' my college landlady had said.

I bet you never thought I'd call you again. Certainly not six years later.

My god, it's so depressing I'm calling you again.

We met once more. On a September weekend at one of the properties she had vacancies in, shaking hands outside a block of six units in Camp Hill — a neat suburb about 15 minutes' drive from the centre of Brisbane. She looked the same: grey hair, wiry, sprightly. A non-nonsense smile with a soft spot for people who proved themselves to be decent.

"I'll give you a 10 per cent discount on the rent," she said, as she showed me through the two options.

I could lease a small renovated one-bedroom flat that didn't get a lot of direct light; or an un-renovated, sunny two-bedroom flat that was still a riot of seventies colours and fixtures. They adjoined each other.

Standing at the rudimentary letter boxes by the road, looking at the open-sided carports underneath each unit, and shared laundry in one corner of the concrete-floored downstairs, I only had one thought looping.

How did it come to this?

I thanked her and took the renovated unit.

Those walls are thin; I hope the neighbours will be quiet.

————

I spent a long time alone on the elevated back landing outside my bedroom door, as I watched the afternoon thunderstorms roll across the city. My view to the sweep of skyscrapers was only broken by a few palm fronds. Big black clouds would rumble in from the west. The television towers on Mt Coot-tha sputtered red warning lights into an ink-pot sky that unleashed oceans. Fat raindrops into sticky air. And I'd be glad I wasn't in the peak hour rush getting through all that water and lightning as the thunder boomed.

By 'storm time' I'd been home for a couple of hours. My shift was 6am–2pm. I summarised radio news and current affairs as I listened to tape recordings made of live bulletins that had been broadcast between 10 minutes and two hours earlier.

When loneliness rose, I often tried to walk it out; to tread it into the warm-baked bitumen. I wandered the dusk-lit suburbs with the smell of jasmine and home-cooked dinners hanging in the humidity. A darkened street became a glimpse of lives through glowing, lamp-lit elevated rectangles and squares — hallways and windows.

Possums rustled from bow to branch and made high-wire silhouettes as they scampered along power lines.

Sometimes I walked until it was too dark to see the bats in the sky. But I felt just as quiet. Just as invisible.

The only thing that got me through my close-to-minimum-wage week was kissing the guy who also worked the early shift. He was a few years younger but taller than me, with an impish grin. He put me in some electro-chemical shock state whenever we touched. We got our hands on as much of each other as we could before anyone else arrived in our small office. He had a girlfriend. We were each other's early morning addiction.

———

Some Sundays I'd drive back to Cleveland to do 'the rounds': all my updates in triplicate, for Dad and his girlfriend; Mum; then Nana and Pop.

Dad and his girlfriend. That just sounds wrong.

*But as long as he's happy, I suppose. I **do** want him to be happy. I know he and Mum both wanted it to work but they had lost their way. Dad's girlfriend seems to mean well but they are like chalk and cheese. She's **nothing** like Mum.*

Maybe that's the point?

I guess the simplest thing to do is just be nice to everyone.

But I don't know what to say to whom. How much do I reveal of the life of each, to the other? I'd never thought about how this would actually work.

Approaching the turn-off to Nana and Pop's place, I had to make a decision.

One day they won't be there to visit. They'd love to see you.

I've just given all my non-existent news twice. It's Sunday afternoon, the weekend is almost over, I need to relax at some point. Before it all starts again. Between groceries and chores and that bloody 4.30am alarm...

You don't have to entertain them; just go in for a few minutes. You in person is better than the few postcards you sent while you were overseas.

But it never is just a few minutes, is it?

I rounded the bend without turning.

I'll visit them next time.

———

My computer at home was set up on a small desk at the window next to the tiny kitchen, its once-advanced CRT monitor pushing back towards the lace curtains. When I had the energy in the evenings or on weekends, I sat looking into that screen and chatted on dating sites with the few men who weren't weirdos. Except when I met them, they *were* weird. Or rude. Or kinky.

I saw one guy intermittently for a couple of months. One night he stood me up at dinner and disappeared. When my phone finally rang, he said, "Sorry, I had an asthma attack that night and I died in the ambulance on the way to hospital."

"You *died*?" I laughed. "Come on — you want to play that card so early? You know you can't top that. What excuse could you possibly use next time? Anyway, that was three weeks ago, what have you been doing since?" I asked.

He clearly expected more sympathy.

Nick told me one of our friends from ships was living an hour away, on the Gold Coast. Jenn had been my initially-prickly assistant photo manager. She was slow to trust but loyal and generous once she did. We'd eaten half of New Zealand together. She said I was the only person she knew who could survive on raisin toast and risotto.

Her Canadian tendency to apologise remained, but so did her candour. She bought me the dating 'how to' best-seller of the time, *He's Just Not That Into You*.

"Sorry, no offence, but I think you need to read it," she said on the phone one night when checking if her gift had arrived in my mailbox.

"Thanks. I think!" I was glad to have another shipmate nearby.

———

Listening to the folksy tunes of The Waifs at home one night, I lay on my stomach, staring into the rug in my small sitting area, my nose just millimetres from the carpet. I sniffed it.

Dusty.

Maybe I could go to Ireland? I can get a visa there until I'm 30, there's still time...

No, I couldn't really face moving again. I can't afford it anyway.

This is not supposed to be my life. I want to be able to go to Barcelona or Reykjavik or Milan for the weekend. To trawl cottages in Surrey with my husband, dreaming of one we might buy. I'm supposed to be married. I hate that leaving him meant leaving half the world behind.

This is awful.

I didn't know how compressed and infuriating life could feel.

Then I remembered the look I used to get from any commuters I'd spoken to on the train about my work, when I went to and from the *Gazetteers* office in between hotel reviewing trips. How the glaze had lifted from their eyes in the moment I suspected they imagined a foreign horizon, and the mix of emotions — regret? bitterness? envy? — when they slipped mentally back into themselves.

Now I'm stuck on one of those trains. Now the vacant stare is mine and there's no station in sight. I had no idea how lucky I was.

I wish I could hit 'fast forward'.

———

Mum came to visit me one weekend. Sunshine peeped across the edge of my kitchen floor.

"You've got the place looking lovely, darling," she tried to be cheerful.

"Thanks, Ma. It's a work in progress," I said.

I made us cups of tea and coffee but I didn't have a balcony to sit on. It was a bit cramped when two of us tried to sit on the landing. So while we talked, I sat at one end of the top step and she sat on the other end of a step a couple lower.

We had no routines for that place.

At one point she was bending to put something in her handbag on the floor, and the rest of her body followed the trajectory downwards until she just sat and wept.

"I feel like my heart is broken into a million pieces," she cried.

I quickly kneeled to put my arms around her. The enormity of her pain hit me for the first time. I berated myself for being so self-absorbed; and I was used to her comforting me. For an instant that role reversal was brutal but I softened into it and I would have given anything in that moment to make her world the bright one she wanted again.

Her tears wet my T-shirt as I rubbed her back. "You'll always have me," I said. My voice cracked on 'have'.

"It's not the same," she said softly.

"I know," I whispered, and we were an island of grief together.

Mum dried her eyes and we sat on my cobalt-blue chaise lounge.

"It's comfy, eh?" she said, blinking back the tears and blowing her nose.

We'd been shopping to set up my flat, and as soon as we'd sat on that couch we thought it was *the one*. It was on sale too.

"Why don't I shout you this now and you can pay me back?" Mum had said. She did and I did, but she forgave the debt halfway through my repayments.

"It's the best lounge ever!" I said with a grin.

Mum sniffed again quietly and found the beginnings of her smile.

———

One February day in Brisbane I turned 28. It was 2006.

That night I had an awkward Thai meal with Mum, Dad and Adam, just down the road from my place. My parents had agreed they'd still mark special occasions together.

Later in the week, two of my neighbours-turned-friends

came out to dinner with me for a girls' night. One had recently divorced, the other had just lost her mother. We were all rebuilding. We still managed a few laughs.

I met Cardiac Guy several weeks afterwards. His messages online had been amusing. He seemed intelligent. He also knew the difference between 'your' and 'you're'.

Points for literacy, Cardiac Guy.

I told him I wanted to meet so I could check he "wasn't a nutter".

He opened the car door for me when he picked me up to take me out to dinner and I was relieved he actually looked like the slim, smiling tall guy in his photo. He listened throughout the meal. He offered to pay — I thanked him but said I'd be more comfortable if we'd split the bill. He asked if I'd like to see him again as we stood on the pavement near his car, illuminated by a street light.

"If you've decided I'm not a nutter, that is," he added.

"I *think* I'm safe," I laughed, "but just to be sure, yes, I would like to see you again. That would be lovely."

He bent his fine frame, full lips and bright eyes towards me. His hand rested lightly on my forearm and he kissed me on the cheek.

"I'll look forward to that," he said as he opened the car door and drove me home. "I'll call you," he said, as I got out.

And he did.

28

One weekend Cardiac Guy and I picked up Naomi from her parents' place in Brisbane and the three of us went out for lunch. It was refreshingly easy to be out and about. Like normal people who didn't feel lost in their own lives.

"Hey, do you guys want to come in?" Naomi asked from the back seat, just as we were pulling up to her folks' again.

He and I looked at each other and I swivelled in the passenger seat so I could face her, "No thanks, we'll head home to mine, I think," I said, smiling.

"Good idea," she agreed, "you two really need to get a room."

We all went to evening ballroom dance class for several weeks in a church hall in Bulimba, in Brisbane's inner east. It was mostly full of middle-aged women. Cardiac Guy enjoyed himself anyway. We cha-cha-ed, samba-ed, and jived our way through the evening; trumpets and maracas pushing through the sound system, onto the street. No one was particularly co-ordinated and we all laughed good-naturedly.

When Cardiac Guy was on the other side of the room one night, Naomi said, "You know you're going to marry him, right?"

All she got from me was raised eyebrows and "you think so, do you?"

He'd often come back to my place afterwards and we'd talk until it was late. He was gentle and quirky, his mind racing well ahead of his rapid speech, with flickering hand gestures to accompany his conversation. His aftershave agreed with me.

You smell good.

A little world sprung up around us when we were together and I was aeons from where I had been in Normandy. I felt safe. I considered what it would be like to feel that way with someone all the time.

Each time Cardiac Guy and I met — after the initial girl-meets-boy nerves — I was at ease.

He was open about the behavioural challenges he faced with ADD and OCD. I read his honesty as bravery, and found the upsides.

Because you work so hard to focus in a conversation, you're a really good listener; being clean and neat is fine with me!

Then: *Bloody hell, Sara, you're not exactly perfect.*

"If things keep going this well, I think you might have to change your surname at some point," he said after dancing one night.

"As in change it to yours?"

"Yes. Though it could get a bit confusing considering my sister is a 'Sarah'...but you know, that would only be until *she* gets married."

"She might want to keep her maiden name."

"She might. But that's not really the point," he grinned.

"Are you serious?"

"Yes."

A family of butterflies caught my stomach. I was diving through a wave. I warmed and relaxed as a sunbather does with the whole of summer awaiting — and I trusted that sensation completely.

Cardiac Guy and I continued to dance and talk and life felt glowing again. Even with my crappy job and no money. I often found myself smiling for no reason.

Seven weeks after we met, he began to ask me to marry him while we were in bed one Saturday morning.

"Stop right there!" I said.

"What's wrong?" he asked.

"No, no, no," I said, getting out of bed and pulling him up, "*last time* someone asked me to marry them was in bed. That can't happen again. We have to *at least* move to the lounge room."

———

"If you have thought about it deeply and he's the one for you, then congratulations, darling."

"Oh. Well, if you're sure, I'm happy for you honey."

"Holy fuck!"

"You look so much happier than you did when you were over here."

"Well... We always knew he'd come home one day and just tell us he'd asked someone to marry him — and here you are! It's lovely to meet you. Welcome to the family."

———

"So, new man, new job, it's all looking up, eh?" said my neighbour one springtime weekend at the clothesline as we hung out our washing. She'd been kind throughout my loneliness, while dealing with her own separation.

"Yes, it is," I said. "It's feeling like the start of a new era, you know?"

"And you didn't even have to go far when you moved in together."

"Yeah, I don't know if the moving guy was glad or annoyed when I told him I was only going to the unit next door!"

Cardiac Guy and I began to find our rhythm in that two-bedroom place, even though it was really only a comfortable size for one person. I bought a large rug to cover the '70s lino in the lounge room; ignored the fittings and revelled in breakfasts in the sunshine.

Our togetherness was a relief. We wore engagement well and had a future to rearrange in the soft haze of weekend sleep-late-together mornings.

I thrilled when *Gazetteers* needed dozens of Australian hotels — and several cities — reviewed. I squeezed those trips into a few short breaks — before starting, and during, my new 9–5 job at a media company. There were properties to visit in Brisbane but I was still made for elsewhere. I flew on assignment to Sydney, Melbourne, Adelaide and Cairns — so grateful to be untethered from a desk; to be anywhere else.

Each ride to the airport pushed me into the world again, lifting me beyond the horizon I'd been so constricted by. There was no queasy ill-ease on those trips; I was at home again on the move. I had purpose. My senses were alive — to the light and smell and architecture and conversations on all the new streets I'd walk.

At each hotel, I had my spiel, my clipboard and my small digital camera. It amused me that a clipboard and good posture could create such an air of authority.

Would I like a tour from the marketing manager? Oh no, that's the last person I want to get held up by. Heard it all before.

"That's so kind of you but actually, it's you I'd like to talk to for a moment," I said to every receptionist who made that offer and the second they wavered: "Don't worry, you're perfectly qualified to help me — besides, you see everything that goes on here — and I *know* you'll know the answers to my questions."

"Okay, if you're sure. I'll do my best."

And when things didn't go my way out on the road, I'd remember the Greek sunshine and Tony and Maureen and the preciousness of their brief annual holiday.

They're trusting me to do this well.

———

A little grief-stricken it was all over again, I realised something at the end of that reviewing contract: the joy of a new relationship aside, my days were actually just reactive; I was mired in a never-ending to-do list.

*How can I make **all** of life exciting again?*

What's it all for, anyway?

I thought I'd found a slice of an answer for the first time, in an early Brisbane summer, when I was 28.

In bed alone one Saturday morning, in soft blooming light before the heat of the day ripened, I lay staring at the wall. The world of a just-finished Paulo Coelho novel was still thick in my senses. 'My' epiphany had been within those pages.

Sometimes you need to go away to come back again; to see home afresh — so you can step into who you truly are.

I folded the idea over and over, like origami. The shape of the final piece only revealed itself slowly.

It was time to admit to the thing I *really* wanted. In doing so, I had to acknowledge there was only one action I could take and the rest was entirely beyond my control. Mum had wanted to do the same thing when she left school; Cardiac Guy was supportive too. Unexpectedly, so was Dad. I thought there would be far too much uncertainty riddling the idea for his liking.

I went for it.

Serendipity, please be kind.

29

I put my bag against the far wall with everyone else, and helped stack the chairs and tables along one edge of the room. When we were finished, we stood in a haphazard scattergun pattern and began to stretch.

After the initial warm up, I gleefully channelled Monty Python and did my own version of a silly walk around the circle, dodging and weaving past others with heads bobbing and arms flailing. But the joke was lost on everybody except the tutor.

"Okay everyone, we'll use the year you were born as the starting point today," said the tutor, "around the room: go."

"1990."

"1989."

In 1989 I was doing Kylie Mole impersonations or crooning The Bangles' 'Eternal Flame' into my hairbrush-as-a-microphone in front of the mirror. 1990 was my awful first year of high school. Oh no, this is how 'When I was your age…' stories start, isn't it?! I'm too young to be doing that!

"1989."

"1990."

"1978."

The collective intake of breath was swift and audible. All eyes shifted to me.

"Oh my god," someone across the room said.

That's a bit rude.

There was a quick follow up though: "*You're* retro!"

Shock and admiration rippled through the drama class. For the first time in my life — at Brisbane's Kelvin Grove campus of the Queensland University of Technology, in 2007 — I was cool.

In the first 20th century drama lecture, the head of the unit proclaimed as she began, "This will be one of the most boring classes you will have. If you are going to break the rules, first you need to understand what they are and where they came from."

Fantastic.

Later that day, I found a spot on the grass with one of the young women I'd sat next to in one of my lectures.

"I'm *so* excited!" she said as we sat down.

"Oh yeah, what about?" I asked.

"Well, now that I'm actually doing this as a degree, I've got a focus. Before I'd just be reading plays, learning about history and going to the theatre — and it wasn't *for* anything, you know? It was all kind of random. Now all my favourite things *mean* something," she paused, looking like she had more energy than she knew how to use. "Does that make any sense?"

"I know *exactly* what you mean," I said. "It's a bit of a long shot, starting to study drama when you're 29, but this is what I wanted to do when I was 18."

"That's awesome!" she said.

"Back then I got a 'proper' degree, but I just wouldn't have forgiven myself if I didn't ever try this."

"Why not?! Full time?"

"No, part time. I also work in government communications. Just started."

She looked puzzled.

"I write media releases and ministerial speeches, that sort of thing. I freelance too, when I can, for travel magazines and stuff."

"Oh, you're a writer. Nice!"

"It has its moments. These days I morph from public servant to drama queen somewhere along George St..."

A few other almost-familiar faces drifted over and joined us cross-legged on the lawn. And I couldn't help thinking sunny days were made for lying on the grass and looking at the clouds and remembering all the things that make us joyful.

I lay there with conversation washing over me, staring skywards, feeling like a kid with keys to a magical kingdom. And I stayed there until the ground felt too cold.

"Okay, I'm gonna head," I said, getting up and trying to shake the grass off my shirt, "see you guys later."

I loved the quiet industry of the library on campus. The smell of books; the crispness of new journals; the hum of photocopiers. Debate and desire pressed into ink — and onto screen and within soundbites — all ready for me to devour.

A hunt for the right shelf for one of the topics of an assignment proved fruitful and I took a stack of books into my arms. A comfy circular orange chair beckoned, warmed in a pocket of sunlight by the window, with a view across treetops. I tucked my right ankle under my backside, put my left elbow on the upholstery, leaned my head upon my hand and began to feast.

———

Brisbane lay sparkling in the winter dark on the other side of Cardiac Guy's windscreen. The gold-orange lights of the Story Bridge slung above suburban rooftops and below the skyscrapers. We were somewhere in the inner east.

"Oh wow, I didn't know this view was here! We have to come back," I said as he descended the hill and moments later the vision was gone.

We were driving a foreign route across town to catch a ferry; navigating only by a brief look at the map before we left home, then by an intuitive draw to water. It was guess work later that evening to retrace our journey exactly.

"This is the street!" I said as we climbed. "Wouldn't it be amazing to live here?"

Before Cardiac Guy could answer, we slowed near the top of the hill, I looked to my left and there, in the shining night out the front of an apartment block, was a 'For Lease' sign.

Fortune, I love you.

I rang the real estate agent the next morning — the apartment was in Hawthorne, about seven minutes' drive from the place Cardiac Guy and I shared; it was at the back of the block of 10, on the top floor. There'd be an inspection the following afternoon.

Cardiac Guy was on call, so I left work early and Dad drove from Cleveland through peak hour traffic to look the place over with me. We arrived ahead of the inspection time and circled the building. The estate agent was late; eventually about a dozen potential applicants followed him up the stairs and we all waited in a straggly, descending line while he fumbled with several sets of keys.

"Wrong keys, sorry folks! Come back tomorrow," he said.

"Well, surely you can go and get the right keys?" I asked. "We've all been waiting here quite some time."

"No, the office is about to close. We'll be in touch to reschedule."

You wouldn't do this for a purchase inspection.

Dad and I fumed.

I went to the estate agent's office the next morning,

mentioned what happened the previous day and requested an inspection and all the application paperwork.

"I am available now, there's no need to bother an agent. I'll just grab the keys and leave my ID here for security, of course, and be back before you know it. I have a feeling it's going to be perfect. If so, we can have a deposit with you by COB tomorrow," I said.

Cardiac Guy and I moved in a few weeks later, in early July.

Jenn kindly sent us towels as a housewarming present — white was a good choice because the kitchen was a modernised version of 1974 and the toilet walls were still wall-papered with flowers. But the 180-degree view across Brisbane was spectacular.

———

A large yellow envelope with an air mail stamp arrived.

Divorce papers.

Petitioner. Respondent.

It's been two years. Are you ever going to send back all my things?

There had been no communication between us for quite a while but I knew that envelope was coming. It was always going to come.

I am not attaching a memory to this.

———

By November, respite seemed elusive. I couldn't switch off. Part-time study plus part-time work gorged on all seven days each week.

Academically I was doing well, but a little witch at work — who would have done Toni proud — was intermittent but persistent with her jibes.

I've been here before; when I can, I'm going to pretend you don't exist. You're a bully and I'm not going to satisfy you by acknowledging you.

Sometimes Cardiac Guy's wall of silence was the loudest sound at 1am, when he was still playing computer games. A memory of Sevenoaks flared: I had lost a man to the screen, again — to war games, to god knows what.

I can't compete with pixels. With guns. Isn't a real-life woman supposed to be the coup? Aren't I interesting enough?

I bought a book about ADD and communication, thinking if I understood more about his world, we would both gain.

"Hey, have you had a chance to look at that book?" I asked, trying to sound casual. "There's some really useful stuff in there."

"Briefly. Some of it reminded me of you," he said flatly.

He wouldn't talk. He wouldn't say much about anything. It made me angry; fierce. Taut and prickly in bursts, I found my tongue and I unleashed truths and not all of them were meant for him.

Each time Cardiac Guy silently looked at me in the aftermath — more resolutely silent than before — I saw the same expression I thought I'd probably worn in Normandy when I couldn't comprehend what, exactly, was wrong with the person yelling; and I couldn't think quickly, I couldn't think at all — and most of all, I *needed* it to stop but I didn't know what to say to make it so.

All the things I'd tried to bury began to float.

And Cardiac Guy and I began to drown.

Why won't you talk to me?

30

E nd of year assessments at uni — theory and practical — had come thick and fast. There was a lot to finish at work too. Soon it would be Christmas.

I still wasn't sleeping well, often half awake for hours, wondering if Cardiac Guy would come to bed.

Maybe it's just as much my fault as it is his?

Wondering.

Maybe I'm depressed or something?

I had never spoken to anyone about my mental health.

I should check that out. I'm not going to cut and run here — we got engaged, for god's sake, that was based on **something***; I'm not going to assume breaking up is the answer.*

In daylight: *What's the difference between a psychiatrist and a psychologist, Dr Google?*

Ah, it seems the essence is that a shrink can prescribe medication.

May as well go the whole hog then. Be efficient about it. I'm not going through everything twice.

The day before my appointment, it occurred to me I should have something written down in case the psychiatrist I'd received a referral to said something like, "So, tell me about why you're here today," as they did in the movies. Then I wouldn't have to think of everything on the spot. So, I wrote:

In the past three-and-a-half years I have:
- married
- separated
- become engaged
- divorced
- moved house 10 times (of which two moves have been international)
- had five different jobs in three different countries
- worked full time, part time and in a home-based office
- begun a second university degree
- started my own freelance business (writing and photography)
- witnessed the separation and divorce of my parents after 29 years of marriage.

This is the first time I have written this down. No wonder I've felt stressed... In a way, the impact of all these events whirls around inside: the elation, anguish, pain, hope, anticipation, disappointment, anger. I am trying to quiet them all and/or extinguish them so I can put my life into a manageable perspective, and not feel overwhelmed.

Three days ago, my fiancé told me he is unsure what he wants in life and whether I'm right for him. I was shocked, angry and frightened. Shocked because he'd not given any serious

indication of these thoughts in the past 18
months. Angry because I felt betrayed; I'd always
stressed that honesty was paramount for me.
Frightened because I don't feel emotionally
equipped to go through another break-up
just now.

In the beige waiting room of the specialists' clinic at a nearby
hospital, I tried not to fidget. Nervy anticipation whirled in my
stomach. I went to the bathroom but worried I'd miss my name
being called. Presumably it wasn't the done thing to
acknowledge anyone else there or wonder about anyone's
particular brand of psychosis and assign dramatic lives and
symptoms to each person. But I couldn't help it.

My name was called.

This is one of those times you want to pretend you're someone else.
But the receptionist already knows you're here.

I've no particular memory of the room I entered, other than
it seemed small, but there was a glimmer of relief when the
doctor wrote something on her notepad and asked me why I was
there. I read the list, with notes, that I'd prepared. I had a bit
more to say, it turned out.

"Sara—," the doctor said, looking up from her notes, "we're
at the end of our session now."

"Oh. Already?" Surely that clock was wrong.

Did I just give a 50-minute monologue?

"Sara, I don't think you're depressed, I think you just have *a
lot* to get off your chest."

She gave me the name of another health professional who
had an office near where I lived, if I ever wanted to talk further.

As I blinked into the harsh summer daylight in the car park,

I was a little stunned but relieved as I called Cardiac Guy with the news. Everything seemed to settle between us then.

———

One February day in Brisbane I turned 30. It was 2008.

I'd reviewed all the top hotels in town for *Gazetteers* and booked one for my small party then overnight stay with Cardiac Guy.

Outside, twilight brought little relief from the thick heat but the plush lobby bar was crisp enough to keep make-up sheen free, and pressed shirts dry. I was a little nervous my disparate groups of guests — singles, pairs and a couple of trios — wouldn't have a good time. Cardiac Guy assured me everything would be fine.

Naomi and Jenn each drove up from the Gold Coast with friends who had also become mine.

"You look so grown up!" Samantha said as we hugged. She'd been back from London for a while and, though she'd rather have played photographer than subject, she smiled for a photo with Mum and another friend, and thankfully the three of them got along well.

Adam and his girlfriend, and Dad — who came solo, at my request — all kept each other company on the other side of the lounge area we all congregated in.

I rounded each small cluster of smiling faces, introducing them to others, sketching the stories and geographies that bound us all.

Everyone seems okay.

Cardiac Guy's parents were kind, as always. They spoiled me too.

Mum and Dad, it's not easy, I know — I'm so glad you're here.

Happiness wound its way through me during dinner at the

adjoining restaurant, as I realised I was sitting at a table with most of the people I loved.

Three nights later, in bed at home and musing on the future now that the big 3-0 had arrived, I asked Cardiac Guy again about what he wanted — in life in general, from his work and relationships. That time, he answered. Haltingly, but fulsomely, and I wondered how long he'd been thinking about it.

I took a deep breath as the sting began.

"You know," I said, "amid all that, there's no room for me."

"No, I guess there isn't," he replied.

And the sting became pain and it was sharper than the last time everything I'd imagined ahead had disappeared.

After we cried, he moved into the spare room.

Not again. I'm not ready yet.

But it was done. We both knew it.

———

In my waking hours, I applied the astringent present-moment focusing mechanism that was bolstered by Jenn's gift of Eckhart Tolle's *A New Earth*. The book's proposition that I remember: our suffering lies in bringing the past — or anticipated future — into 'now'.

*I am putting marmalade on my toast. I'm eating breakfast as I look across the waking suburbs. Dew is still wet on the oval, runners are misting breath into the morning. There is nothing sad in **this** moment.*

*I am on my lunch break, on the office rooftop, and the sun feels good on my skin. There is nothing sad in **this** moment.*

*I am sitting on a ferry looking at the water. There is nothing sad in **this** moment.*

There were months of that, as I went to work and uni and

rehearsals, and tried to shoe-horn myself into an endless present. But there were fewer distractions at night.

I continued to dream of Normandy. Visions that swelled deep within the darkness and dreams that rocked me in the half-waking time before sunrise. I was always trying to return. My mind tunnelled into another place to concoct those journeys by land, sea and air. By scheming and bargaining — with mix'n'match baggage of promise and peace and regret.

Two things were usually the same in the dreams: I'd sense I was close to the cottage but I never had a map, and the faceless others who were with me couldn't help — so I couldn't get there. Or, I was determined to reach the cottage but the closer I got, the more obstacles were thrown my way — natural disasters, physical danger, emotional deal making — so I couldn't get there.

Just once in many years of dreaming did I find my way back to that house in the field in Northern France. It was as if no one had been there for 1,000 years. The emptiness was crushing.

31

The theatre company director was a fierce blonde with a scrappy wild streak whose voice had become like steel one winter morning.

"You always have a choice, Sara," she said as we sat at a cold aluminium table in a brick courtyard. Insipid sunshine failed to warm us.

"I'm really sorry, I just can't finish the volunteer placement with you. I need to take on more work; I have rent and…" my voice trailed off as the angry tears threatened. I wiped my clammy hands on my jeans.

"You could have chosen to keep your commitment and gotten the money from somewhere else," she said.

"There is no 'somewhere else'," I replied, "it's just me."

It's just me now.

"You could have asked me for a loan." She had snake's eyes.

"No, I don't do that sort of thing. I pay my own way. I'm sure you'll find someone else to help you out. Sorry," I repeated, as I got up to leave.

'You always have a choice, Sara.' It rang in my head for years.

Sprawled on my couch a few weeks later, the lounge room drenched in sunset gold, I dialled Mum's number.

I said things like, "You don't have much control over an acting career — you're always at the mercy of someone else, you know? Do you have the right look? It's so subjective... And success in one play doesn't mean it will keep happening... I could spend years trying and have nothing to show for it... I don't want to live like a student anymore — now or later..."

Mostly, I ached for the world again. Everything that was happening beyond my days, in other time zones. Everything I couldn't quite reach. Mum understood that too.

Afterwards my ear burned from the long press of the phone.

I looked at nothing in particular but heard the activity at the oval a few streets away.

Footy training.

When the memory of improv class bounded in, I pushed it away. But it danced right back, centre stage. I'd been tantalised in that classroom, chairs and tables shuddering as we cleared them to the boundaries; when we lost ourselves in a space that wasn't real but weightier than fancy. Together, relative strangers, we built worlds and spun stories and lived lifetimes in three hours. One prompt: "It's England in 1887. You've just been arrested..." Another: "You're on a mission to Mars and a warning light in your spacecraft has just illuminated..." I always left awed; a little breathless, with the emotions of a conjured character rattling under my skin. A kick at making the very air come alive.

I'd succumbed to an exquisite thrill when I'd discovered NASA had an artist-in-residence program; when I heard Philip Glass's music for the first time, enveloping a full silent lecture theatre in which everyone had forgotten to breathe.

But none of that mattered anymore. The phone call to Mum had been a postmortem. I'd just left university; 18 months into my drama degree. Halfway; they'd given me credit for previous studies.

Whistles blew down at the oval and the lights blazed above the steaming football players as the evening air brittled.

Embarrassing as it is to admit, I don't think I'm a very good actor. If I'm really honest, I thought I might uncover a natural talent. And it would somehow save me.

I can always just go to the theatre — I don't have to be in the play.

With the full-time hours on offer at work, I could actually go on holiday. I haven't had a holiday since...2004, when Mum came to visit the UK. Four years ago.

It's time to grow up; not everyone gets what they want.

Then I heard the fainter voice: *But that was my last big wish.*

———

Daybreak seeped around the edges of my closed curtains one Monday morning in October. I'd already been awake in bed to see the night melt into lilac light, then amber; the churn of my stomach too familiar. Trying to sleep despite it — *over* it, *instead* of it — in vain.

It's just first-day nerves. You've had loads of first days, done it all before, you'll be fine.

The birdsong rang out for a couple of hours after sunrise.

By the time I actually got up, cars had been filing over the bridges I could see — the Gateway and the Story Bridge — for a while.

I tried to wash the nerves away in the shower. Shampoo and soap disappeared down the drain but I still wore a cloak of knots — my skin was just cleaner.

The dining table wouldn't stay still. Breakfast was a more-woozy-making affair: plain toast with a wisp of butter, too much.

The faintest odours, pungent. At one point, I had to hold onto the edge of the table. It wasn't that I was dizzy, as such, but the world seemed to move without me.

What was I thinking? It's only a four-week contract.

Don't think about that now, you've got to get there first. Eat a bit more or you'll feel worse later.

I ran to the bathroom, not sure which end of my body would violently expel its contents first. The mop bucket was already sitting on the floor by the toilet; I grabbed it as I sat down and wretched.

My second shirt for the morning became doused in perspiration. I was shaking. There was no lifeline, just my own voice. Just the conversation in my head.

If you're going to make the ferry, you have to go in a few minutes.

I can't. It will have to be the next one.

What are you worried about, anyway? You know how to do this job; it's the same, just different people.

It's a promotion.

So? It'll be fine. Actually, it won't be if you don't go.

I can't keep going through this. I can't do this. I can't do this anymore.

I cleaned up and changed outfits. Again. I abandoned the idea of breakfast and sat on the edge of the couch for a moment.

Brisbane, sunny Brisbane in 2008, outside. I had to do that sometimes, say the name of the city I was in — and the year — it was a broader anchor in the arc of life, a precursor to the present moment focus.

Brisbane, 2008.

All the other commuters were dashing outside. I couldn't even contemplate momentum — my balance, my bowels, my stomach all raged. My body was trying to get out of itself; my mind, like a kite, tethered: present *and* away.

What am I going to do? I don't think I can run for the bus. God, make this stop. I'll believe in you if you can make it stop. This battle is too much.

Deep breath.

In. Out.

Slower.

In. Out.

Deeper.

In. Out.

Shoulders down.

In. Out.

I need some water.

My hand shook the glass; I carefully drank the little ripples.

Let them know you'll be late to work. Tell them you're sick. It's not a good look but you can't do anything about it now.

Maybe I won't go.

You have to.

I can't talk to anyone just now.

You have to do it soon or they will think you're not coming.

I just...

This is stupid. There's nothing wrong with you. Get yourself up and out that door. You're a professional.

I can't... I have to...

I ran to the bathroom.

At the electric edge of my nervous system, in some Morse code kind of spasm, a single thought shot into the condensing darkness I imagined: *Is this what it feels like to go mad?*

The sun warmed my back as I sat on the toilet, head bowed into a bucket, and I had to rally all the unruly parts of me — essentially everything — to make it, presentably, outside.

Even as I drove to the ferry, and circled for so long to park, hands perspiring on the wheel — *I'm here too late; I'm too late for a spot* — the world felt like it was existing without me. I was a hologram of myself as I walked several minutes, as quickly as I could, to the wharf.

The queue was still long and trailed a couple of dozen metres through the park then wound parallel to the road, past an old Moreton Bay fig. Waiting in that line, spent before I even got to the river, time became a little wormhole, crunching and gnawing on memories and dreams and each moment that coiled around the second hand of my watch.

Mum and Dad gave me this watch for Christmas 1987, when I was nine. I remember unwrapping it at Nana and Pop's place...

I entered a government building in the city that I'd walked past countless times before, about 10am. Without a security pass, I had to ask the guard on the desk to phone upstairs to my new boss. She came down to meet me.

After our slightly stilted but pleasant conversation in the lift, we rounded a corner to a small pod of about six desks and she introduced me to the communications team. A highly-experienced handful of ex-journalists; mostly women, one young man. Everyone was concerned. Strangers, new colleagues, were genuinely worried about me being all right.

I smiled, with a dismissive wave of my hand, "Oh, it's probably nothing — I think I ate something a bit dodgy. Sorry I'm late. Is this me?" I motioned to an empty desk and, at confirmation, put my handbag down, tried to quell my embarrassment and ignore my hunger and all that whirled within. "So, who can I help, with what?"

32

Two days later, I stuck a wedding invitation I'd just received on my fridge. The magnet made a satisfying *clunk* — and I stared at the paper for a long while. *New Zealand. Just near Auckland. Late November: six weeks away. Perfect!*

I hadn't seen Melissa or James since they let me stay with them on my last night in the UK, more than three years earlier. I wanted to go to their wedding.

I don't think I can go.

Of course you can. New Zealand's just a hop, skip and a jump, remember?

Charlotte was going to be flying out from Canada for it and I hoped Naomi could come. It would be like our London days again.

Why is this so hard? It's a wedding invitation — that's wonderful! I just don't think I can.

It was time to make a call.

My peppermint tea was too hot to sip. I'd finished filling in my questionnaire and the painting on the waiting room wall disturbed me. The picture looked innocuous: sand, umbrellas, waves, blue skies.

Something is wrong with that image but I can't work out what it is.

"Hi Sara, come on through," The Counsellor said. I was only a few streets away from my apartment; I held onto that.

*What if there is something **really** wrong with me? I'm a creative person, I need my mind. It's my life. What if I could just live happily in denial?*

I picked up my handbag and my tea. I sat on her couch in the spare but welcoming room as she closed the white wooden door gently behind me. She smiled as she sat in an armchair opposite. I crossed and uncrossed my legs. And crossed them again. Late afternoon sunshine skirted the edges of the large window behind her. Through it I could see a paling fence and the edge of a tree.

"So, I know it sounds silly," I said, "but I've just received an invitation to a friend's wedding and I really want to go but I just don't think I can."

The Counsellor said, "Tell me more about that," and I let go.

I told her all about the new full-time job I'd started earlier that week; how it was all chance: it was a promotion, it allowed me to get away from a nasty former colleague, but it was only a one-month contract.

I'll have to pray they keep extending it.

I recounted the first morning, days earlier, trying to get out the door, and how I feared I was breaking very slowly.

Or maybe not slowly at all.

"Everything eased after a few hours," I said, "after the introductory rounds at work, I was just left with wild hunger pangs and new-starter administration. Two days later —

yesterday, when I called you — my friend's wedding invitation arrived."

The Counsellor wasn't taking any notes.

How are you going to remember all this?

"You know, anxiety is a natural and healthy emotion," she said when I stopped for a moment. "It keeps us from danger, allowing us to sense threats and act accordingly."

"You mean the 'fight or flight' response?"

"Yes. But when we're on alert all the time, and our brain reads everyday situations as threats, that's when it becomes a problem," she said.

Anxiety.

She made some analogy about soldiers and war zones and I dropped into a sea of memory.

Dad's speech about the jungle in Vietnam: the smell, the nimbleness of the enemy, how heightened that world was at the precipice of life. How he always instinctively ducked when there was loud thunder overhead.

Me as a teenager, never wanting to go to school — almost being ill each morning, for so many years.

Later, flying into San Francisco en route to my first cruise ship, the world had skewed. Nauseated, perspiring and suddenly silent, I'd closed my eyes and willed that plane to the ground.

I relived the dash back to the bathroom when The Englishman had come to pick me up at the Royal Sailors' Home Club at 6am when we were driving to London.

And in one fire blast of crystallised memory from a dead winter night in Normandy, I heard The Englishman appealing: "There's something you're not telling me. What is it? What are you hiding from me?"

"Nothing! I'm not hiding anything from you."

It had been the truth.

I had no unifying language or concept for what had been

happening to me intermittently for years. Sometimes fleeting and sometimes roaring, there had been no coagulation of its variants in my mind; no pattern I could find. It shape-shifted just enough to remain elusive.

For the first time — when I was 30 — it had a name: anxiety.

"The worst thing about anxiety is that it robs you of experiences in life," The Counsellor said, "but *you're* the one who can control it. My sense is it will take you practice and continued exposure to events that prompt your anxiety before you can get through the discomfort, but the first step is being aware of what's happening."

She came to know as much of me as there was to know. Everything charming and spiteful; everything fearful and aspiring and absurd. The corpses of my secrets were laid bare and catharsis shored up all that was set to crumble.

I guess I have to look at it. Right into the face of the very thing that makes me feel like I'm broken.

———

Sadie and I still emailed. It had been four years since I'd seen her; seven years since we worked at sea together. I wrote to her in LA.

 These days I seem to be subconsciously consumed by the possible pitfalls of even going out for a drink or dinner with a new person... Somewhere along the way I just shut down and got scared and found getting out of my comfort zone a bit traumatic.

So I've been having difficulty looking forward to the wedding I'm going to in New Zealand on the weekend. I leave on Thursday, and I'm doing better today — friends to see and fun to be had and all that. I'm trying to get into the "Bring it on!" mindset, rather than thinking of all the things that could go wrong.

I'm telling myself that it's friends I'll be with for the next six days, and if I have a problem (feeling ill or whatever) and I can't quite cope for a minute or an hour, I'll just tell them why. I don't want to hide my anxiety anymore, that's what keeps making it difficult, I think. Only you and my parents know.

———

Charlotte's 'four-month bump' was almost camouflaged by her floral bridesmaid dress. I was beetroot-faced, having explored Auckland that day with an old friend from *Gazetteers*, without adequate sunscreen. But we gave the camera cheesy grins in the late afternoon, hinterland vineyards draped over rolling hills behind us.

Mel was due to arrive soon.

A cluster of guests eagerly hushed at the entrance to the reception venue as shiny black cars with tinted windows rolled up the driveway. It was several minutes before Mel emerged. When she did, she looked radiant; James, steadfast and proud.

I couldn't help the catch in my throat and misting eyes as I hugged them.

"It's so good to see you," I said. "I'm so happy for you both. And Mel, I have no words."

As twilight became night and stars appeared, I'd never felt such love in one room. It held together all the hearts that wanted to break: Mel's parents had flown to New Zealand for the wedding but her dad died the day before it.

We could only try to bring all the joy we had, to make the hole a tiny bit lighter for that one, special evening.

*Thank god I got on that plane. **This** is the world right here; all its grief and celebration. This is love.*

Around 1am, while Charlotte and I were waiting for a taxi back to the city, I felt it. And I began to practise what I'd run through with The Counsellor.

What, exactly, am I physically feeling right now?

I'm shaking a little.

Take a deep breath. What are you thinking about the shaking?

It reminds me of the shudder — the awful sensation I feel when I vomit. I'm worried that might suddenly happen.

Is there any evidence that could be true?

Not really; I don't think so.

If it did turn out to be true, what could you do?

Well, if it happened before the taxi arrived, there are bathrooms just down the hall.

And if it happened after the taxi arrived?

I guess I'd just have to ask the driver to pull over and I'd have to be ill by the side of the road.

Take a deep breath. Try to keep your breathing even. Relax your body. Is there another reason you might be shaking?

Well, it has gotten cooler now; it's the middle of the night and I'm in a summer dress.

So perhaps you're just cold?

I guess so...Yes, I think that's it. I'm just cold!

33

M idnight over the Caspian Sea. Four years of reorienting brought me back to you, belly of an aeroplane en route to London.

I was 31. It was July 2009.

In your hurtling, liminal space, I was a little scared of the self I might find lingering when we landed.

Could there be some sort of torn twin waiting? One I couldn't comfort?

Water and shadow lands below eased the ochre burn on my brain from your seat-back screen. *Wake in Fright,* the 1971 Australian desert thriller, had lured my senses away from sleep and into the Never Never. While watching, I decided I would follow the whispers west of Australia's Great Dividing Range. How and when, I didn't know.

I've never been to the Outback. There's still so much of my own country to see.

And I was doing it again, still: putting myself in two places. But you, flying machine, knew I was only ever buckled into one.

You held me — held *us*, aloft. A collection of the curious, strong, bereaved, exhausted, wealthy, stoic, ambitious and fresh-wailing specimens of humanity. Not quite here, not quite there. Streaking through a fragile shell of atmosphere, every breath a marvel.

————

Quiet in the shadows of St Paul's Cathedral for a while, I stood in the same place I had in 2005 when I was shedding a life.

It's okay. We wrap ourselves up and move on and it's really all right.

I hesitated to leave.

As if I needed to be standing in a certain spot to bring about some sort of internal or metaphysical crisis, I circled the building, pausing a few times. Nothing felt amiss. Watched by gargoyles and angels as I looked across the River Thames, time closed itself. I was whole — and my memory of that other time just an echo in the vast metropolis.

*Is it **really** okay?*

Yes.

My holiday began in earnest when two trains and a taxi took me west.

North Devon's coastal cliffs were among England's highest — hiding coves below and topped by trails. Flora welled from a spell book: small hare's ear, purple gromwell, autumn squill and clustered clover. In a cliff-top tea room, with a fresh brew and clotted cream on my scones, I settled.

It was dismal outside but my brighter memories of that hemisphere doused me. I layered place upon place in my mind, gossamers of geography and sensation, looking for the essence of each.

An upset stomach at the same café left me shot through with anxiety. Panicky and perspiring I went to the pharmacy and a smiling attendant patted the back of my hand as she dispensed a small packet of pills.

"You've travelled half the globe; you're in a strange place. The food is different — not to mention the weather! — it happens, pet."

Breathe. There's no real threat here. You're okay; you're just on the bus. You'll be back at the cosy hotel room soon. It's only 25 minutes.

The next morning, the hotel owner kindly gave me a lift to a farm up the road. I stepped out into mud as a man in gumboots came to greet me. I didn't gush, "You're my second-favourite author and I'm so excited to meet you!" as I'd feared. It was slightly worse.

I offered my hand. He shook it. I blurted, "Hi Tom, I'm Sara, lovely to meet you. You know, when I got The School of Life newsletter, I changed my flights from Australia at the last minute to come — I can't wait!"

He gave a short laugh.

Oh god, I sounded all 'fan girl'.

I was enamoured with the notions Tom Hodgkinson's books extolled about paring life to its basics in a sumptuous way: taking care with food and community, ideas and daydreaming; keeping central the heart of what it was to be human.

That morning, about a dozen people — mostly Brits; many of whom were camping in Tom's soggy back field for a couple of nights — stood in the farm's ramshackle garden, under rain-threatening skies. Tom's talk of scholars and sustainability was peppered with anecdotes about his arrival in Devon with his young family from London, and the pity a few locals had taken upon them, after watching his months of graft in the soil.

"What you need," his new neighbours had said, "is a mattock."

I thought everyone knew what a mattock was but I was wrong. Osmosis during childhood had gifted me more than I realised and I had to look at the ground as I stifled a smile during the mattock-wielding demonstration.

Time slipped through my jet-lagged, slightly wrought wiring.

Night came: a candle-lit banquet table in an old village hall, a simple feast — the smiles of strangers in a golden glow; mellowing conversation.

Morning: a handful of people gathered around a farmhouse kitchen table, the smell of baking bread in the air.

Later: chairs in a circle, a small group talking about Stoic philosophy and German poetry with an ease I wanted.

Bonus: I found a few people with fiery, curious minds I wanted to keep knowing.

I didn't go wild swimming below the cliffs off the squally coast. There's 'simple living' and there's 'slightly mad'.

After email addresses were swapped and everyone began to re-scatter throughout the British Isles, on a whim, I decided to detour via an old haunt in Somerset before heading back to London.

"Well, you're a long way from home," I said to a stranger with an Australian accent in an Akubra hat, at a bed-and-breakfast in Bath.

"Yeah, by the sounds of it, so are you?" the man replied with a good-natured grin.

Tony and his wife, Meredith, were Outback farmers. Out the back o' Bourke. Our breakfasts were chatty. He gave me his card.

"If ever you're out our way..." he said.

Serendipity, you sly dog.

"I have to tell you, I have a habit of taking people up on their invitations, so please don't say I'm welcome to visit unless you truly mean it," I said.

"Of course! Come out any time."

Their invitation buoyed me because I couldn't find the Bath I remembered — except for the old map shop.

Time was up.

After a couple of days with friends in London, a train whisked me north. Up the spine of England, through places I'd never known. The happiness of wandering swelled in my chest; the smallest details from every day were an enchantment.

In a railway tunnel somewhere near Leeds was a patch of graffiti: 'Albert the kid is ghosting'.

Scotland. Edinburgh penetrated me — all urgent and brooding and sandstone and shadows. Like it was a city that could inhabit and rewire a personality. Legends were boiled into the rock the castle was built upon. Old Town closes spidered their way down the hill, their subterranean histories almost lost. I felt some echo of the battle and bloodshed boiled into the soil.

The Writers' Museum honoured Robert Burns, Sir Walter Scott and Robert Louis Stevenson. "To travel hopefully, is a better thing than to arrive," Stevenson once said.

That's not always true.

Mum's tales of Edinburgh from five years earlier, flourished anew in my mind.

In the Scottish Highlands' tiny former spa town of Strathpeffer, I walked in the pine shadows made by the last of the sun, lungs loaded, almost content.

But really, I was being too swift. Again. Wanting too much: trying to drink in a blur of mountains, lochs and foxgloves — it was achingly superficial but all I could do. I'd saved for a year, and waited for so many more to be there. I consoled myself with photos and written fragments, vowing to return.

In a week, I'd be back in Brisbane.

A BBC radio play about Dylan Thomas engrossed me as I drove, alone, through the wild country. The radio spilled the poetry and prose of heartbreak. I stopped by a mountain near

Fort William. It seemed a giant thing from a fairytale land. It proudly pushed into growling low-slung clouds that were hovering above an iridescent golf course.

I was so tired — I'd driven almost 1,300 kilometres (808 miles) in five days, looking for last-minute accommodation each night.

I truly stopped, for the first time.

Life got bigger around me. It was part truth and part illusion, my vision raced as though it continued to trace the road ahead. I turned the radio off. Letting the silence pool, I tried not to drown in it. Rain spat on the windscreen. Clouds hugged closer to the glowering mountain.

The Counsellor's voice drifted into my mind, she'd said something like: "People with anxiety often have poorly-developed self-soothing mechanisms. You have to find a way to calm yourself and not always look to others."

I cried splotched, heaving tears with my head resting on my hands on the steering wheel.

Wanderlust had made me achy — again. My life bent to the habit because there was nothing else. And even when there had been, my appetite for the horizon was unsated.

I was a wanderer. Perhaps I always would be.

That's the truth. Let it in.

I want to scream in the face of everyone who tells me 'You have to settle down sometime'.

I know you do.

But, I don't know how to make a life like this.

Keep going. Keep looking.

*I don't know what I'm looking **for**.*

Keep going.

34

"Hey man... Yeah I'm on the plane, we're waiting to get off... You know what? I'm getting married too... Yep, I asked her... Well, I made the mistake of mentioning it to my aunt — she talked me into it — I said I couldn't ask 'cause I didn't have a ring, then she gave me a ring that was my grandmother's and I thought 'Well I gotta do it now'... We were at this place and she was standing on a stone wall looking at the sunset... We went back there two days later and the wall she'd been standing on had crumbled... After I asked her to marry me I went into the deepest depression. I didn't say a word for 20 minutes. I felt like my dog had died. And you know, I get claustrophobic, so all this time we've been flying I've been trying to breathe and forget about being in a plane. And this bit now? It nearly kills me. The sheer anticipation of getting off and not being able to — this is my nightmare."

The owner of those words had been in the row behind me.

Who does that? Who says that? Does the woman have any idea? I get you on wanting to get off the plane though.

The voice of a freshly-coiffed and perfumed British Airways flight attendant hailed from the public-address system.

"We wish you a very warm welcome to Los Angeles."

———

Sadie and I filled her studio apartment in Hollywood with soundbites meant to plug the holes between our emails and build the five years since we'd seen each other into something more complete. However long or short, our conversations were tinkerings — trying to build life like a Meccano set.

Maybe this bit is meant to go here...

Or great imaginings: "Wouldn't it be amazing if...?"

Her cat tried to sleep on my face at 3am.

"Kai, not now," I said groggily as I gently nudged the cat aside, my sneeze almost instantaneous. She curled near my head and purred and I stroked her for a few minutes, missing having pets after growing up with so many. But my sinuses launched their great rebellion and it continued beyond the early hours of the morning.

When it was light and Sadie and I we were both vaguely coherent, though our expressions and hair suggested otherwise, I told her about Kai's attempted new sleeping arrangement.

"Aw, that means she likes you," Sadie said.

I sneezed again; my head was full of incessant itchy-scratchiness.

"Oh no," I said, blowing my nose.

"What's wrong?" Sadie asked.

"I'm pretty sure it's the fur."

"But you're not allergic to cats."

"I know, it's like a bad hay fever thing, or there's *something* here my body isn't liking," I said with stinging eyes, before I blew my nose again. I wanted to rip my own face off, "I'm so sorry but I think I'll have to get some drugs and go to a hotel."

"Oh."

"I don't think this is going to settle without some serious antihistamines. Don't worry, I'll find a place nearby, and we'll still hang out, of course. That's why I'm here!"

"Okay..."

—————

At the crack of a mid-August mid-morning, Sadie picked me up from a few blocks away and we set out for Santa Barbara.

"We can pretend we're on a road trip," I said with a grin.

"We *are* on a road trip," Sadie countered. She put snacks in the console between us after getting fuel.

I think we mentioned *Thelma & Louise* and a better ending, and I was relieved we slipped into an easy quiet as the Mini Cooper hummed north along Highway 101. The flawless Pacific stretched in an arc of postcard-blue on our left; the dry hills to the right reminded me the desert winds didn't have far to blow to reach the Californian coast.

A cool breeze did little to disrupt the sea-sprayed waterfront in Santa Barbara. The summer air seemed to whisk away lingering jet lag and I was grateful for the pharmacist who'd directed me, the day before, to the salve for my sinuses.

Sadie and I wandered in the sun to the beach, along the pier. Past coloured umbrellas and sandcastles and a bike hire stall with 'Rent Fun!' emblazoned on its flyers. At the sight of the flyer, we turned and said to each other at the same time:

"That's what we've been missing!" and "We've just been doing it wrong!"

We stopped giggling to gorge on lunchtime pizza with other camera-toting tourists.

There was something else Sadie wanted to see while we were on our day-trip and it sounded interesting.

From the outside, Santa Barbara Mission was arches and

whitewashed- and pale-stone walls with terracotta-tiled roofs and a soaring, cross-topped church flanked by cacti. It reminded me of the history that had been outlined on a sign I'd seen in the waterfront park in Monterey years earlier.

At the edge of the large parking lot I took a few frames of the exterior, and the long black streak of westward-heading road that ran right past piqued my interest.

Next time.

If we weren't already recognisable as tourists, we clinched it by stopping at the entryway to photograph each other with our chin resting atop a wooden cut out with the body of a monk in a brown robe painted on it.

The cloisters rimmed an immaculate cottage-like courtyard garden — roses and lavender among the flowers; a neat lawn; a central fountain; sunshine bathing palm trees too. A wall display of the original tools used by the first inhabitants fascinated me; a fading painting of a resurrected Jesus hung by a blue-shuttered window; there were so many plaques in the crypt; tree roots had corrupted plots and headstones in the cemetery.

As the two of us took our separate but similar paths through the monastery — no apologies needed for any exorbitant time in one place, circling one object, getting just the right light — a familiar welling of calm began. And it lit the corners of my sinewed mind that had been so dark only days before; all the brighter for being out on the road, all the stronger then for having someone to share it.

———

When Hollywood Boulevard was awash with late afternoon light, I walked alone amid the tourist hustle and relaxed into my stride.

An impersonator from *KISS*, with crazy hair and trademark

black and white make-up, had removed his prosthetic tongue and was sucking on a cigar instead, as he slouched in a chair outside the Coffee Bean and Tea Leaf café. Across the road, Freddy Krueger was looking distinctly dispirited as he leaned against a wall near Madame Tussaud's. Pocahontas was enthralled by her mobile phone.

From the northern side of the Hollywood and Highland Center was an unfettered view of the Hollywood sign. From the southern side, I had a birds-eye view of break-dancing street performers encircled by a clapping crowd. Everyone's enthusiasm boomed as a fire truck pulled up, and the firemen clapped and made brief bursts of the siren in time with the performers' music.

The nearby open-air fountain had been shut off for the night, leaving wet, half-expectant children in it, squealing, wanting to keep playing in the water that had sprung magically from the ground.

A beggar on the corner sat still and quiet.

Dusk was coming.

An attractive man behind a café counter bantered with me.

"Are you Scottish?" he asked.

"Australian," I smiled.

"I'm American — so I can't tell!" he smirked, "But thank you for the *Mad Max* movies. And thank you for Heath Ledger — the best Joker ever."

With my green tea in-hand, I rounded the corner onto North La Brea Ave. Two men in their mid-twenties were walking in front of me, speaking an Eastern European-sounding language. One handsome; the other exceedingly plain. I imagined a tableau of the two in a bar.

What would it be like to be the friend of the guy who always got the girl? To put all that extra effort into conversation with no guaranteed result? Or perhaps the plain looking one was actually thoroughly charming and he was glad to have his mate along because it gave him a head start attracting the ladies... Or the men...

Through the open window of an apartment up to my left, I heard someone washing up; someone else within the same building yelled a couple of words I didn't catch.

Stepping into a narrow band of sunlight that managed to squeeze between buildings, I looked to my left and two cyclists were riding along a tree-lined street, so quiet by comparison to the boulevard just two blocks away. The cyclists had the easy manner of friends who were comfortable in their surroundings, chatting as they rode.

I noticed all those things quickly — then imagined the people just a little way down the street washing their clothes and waiting on the spin cycle at the laundromat. Everyone just going about their business. Talking with friends, riding their bikes, walking on the street, doing their laundry.

It felt so good to be out in the last light of the day, far from home, where people were playing out their own grand stories — just accretions of everyday things.

*Life lives in **these** moments.*

Sometime later, I scrawled into my notebook and this came out almost whole:

> *These are the words that shall carry me home*
> *When I have strayed far from the path*
> *Through the forest of night, wrapped in solitude tight*
> *Fighting shadows both thick-set and sharp.*
>
> *These are the words that shall carry me home*
> *When adrift on a rough, boundless sea*
> *As waves lash with spite, and there's no land in sight*
> *No beacon or buoy, just a plea.*

These are the words that shall carry me home
When I'm kneeling below the church spire
My eyes to the skies, trying not to despise
The mud that's adhered from the mire.

These are the words that shall carry me home
When home seems like so long ago —
It's since rained on my soul, I've been broken and cold
And wandered with nowhere to go.

These are the words that remind me I'm home
For my true home is deep within me:
In the absence of two, to create one anew
I've forged my own warm sanctuary.

It's a space I've made bright with love that I've known
That's criss-crossed the whole of my life
From all 'round the world, I've sweet memories furled
As daughter and best friend and wife.

So now it's just me, but I'm not alone
And these are the words that shall carry me home.

PART V

BIRTHPLACE | 2009–2013

AGE: 31–35

35

Australia, four months later

t the end of spring, I abandoned my latest desk for a week. There were people I had to see.
I drove.

Beyond the fuzzy limit of Brisbane metro radio, for 183 songs, with great thought-spooling chunks of silence once my iPod was emptied. The towns I swept through arced down a floodplain from southern Queensland to the western interior of New South Wales: Warwick, Goondiwindi, Moree, Walgett, Brewarrina. A mouthful of Anglo and Aboriginal names.

Into the Outback.

At first the landscape held straw-coloured grass and wheat fields; flashes of burnt orange for tussocks and dust; sky a storm-cloud blue with daubs of a lighter shade for distant mountains. It felt more desolate and desiccated the further I went.

The smells wafted or thumped through my half-open window: fertiliser, silage, wet soil, road kill.

Nina Simone crooned *Stompin' at the Savoy* in a particularly uninspiring stretch of empty country somewhere near Moree. I laughed.

Guess I've been on my own a while now.

Views to the front and rear revealed the bitumen hammock I was buzzing along in, strung between two ever-moving horizons. It was easy to speed.

Bourke emerged from seemingly endless grassy plains dotted with mulga, saltbush, black box and coolibah trees.

A town of roughly 3,000 — set on the banks of the Darling River that spilled and shrank with the wrenching cycle of flood and drought — the history of the place ran deep and wide too. A heady entwining of folklore, fact, and poetry. Bourke Shire was the size of Denmark.

Scatterings of frangipani, palms and jacaranda trees were unexpected and homely. But the shuttered shops on the main street hinted at an underbelly. Many had been down on their luck before — and still were — in that town, but its heyday brought one mighty boom. Bourke had once been one of the largest inland ports in the world.

I arrived in its 10th year of drought.

"Are you a tourist?" asked a young Aboriginal girl as I looked at the assortment of local maps and information behind glass on the wall of Bourke's former train station.

"Yes," I said, smiling.

"Where did you come from?"

"Brisbane."

"Where's that?"

"It's nearly 1,000 kilometres (600 miles) away."

"Is that, like, out of Australia?" she wondered, nose wrinkling.

My new friend was an 11-year old who liked Bourke because she could "ride and walk all over, not like in the cities".

I just had 10 more kilometres (6 miles) to drive. I almost

missed Tony and Meredith's driveway but thought I'd probably been skirting their land for a while: they farmed sheep, cotton and wheat across two properties covering 15,000 hectares (37,000 acres).

A chance meeting on the other side of the world brought me here. From Bath to Bourke. That's got a ring to it.

"Oh, I just need to check the oven," said Meredith, "I wanted to make something nice for dinner tonight." She proudly put a salmon quiche on the bench to cool. My stomach knotted and I flushed with embarrassment and regret.

"I'm so sorry, I don't eat seafood. You've gone to so much trouble and I feel awful. I didn't think to mention it," I said.

"Oh. Okay. Well, we'll figure out something. More for Tony!"
I'm the worst guest.

Tony was a little embarrassed I'd taken a photo of the trampoline and cubby house in the dust of what used to be a garden around their home.

"Yes, we're a little sensitive about our garden — it used to be lovely — but by the end of 2000 it was all dead," he said.

Meredith spoke almost wistfully about gardens she'd seen in town.

We ate dinner on placemats that were laminated sheets of coloured scribblings, drawn many years ago, by the couple's three kids. Family photos through the ages adorned the walls and the fridge. Though away at school and overseas, the children's presence was strong. So was Tony's desire to dismiss any romantic notions I might have of the bush.

"This is not *McLeod's Daughters*. The fact is it's really tough," he said.

Tony and Meredith had come to Bourke in 1993 with a young family — determined to create their own business on the back of 'the mighty Darling' — after land was difficult to wrestle from generational family farming where they'd grown up, near Moree.

"The first six years were really great. We invested in infrastructure and put processes in place; then the drought came," Tony said. "We've also lost 67% of our water allocation through government legislation and we'd built the place up based on the original allotment of water."

I wondered how they continued when people they knew had committed suicide during the devastation of drought and bankruptcy.

"If I sat here thinking how bad things were and how much money I've lost, well…" Tony's sentence hung in the air. "You just can't let it get to you."

Known in the area as advocates for and users of innovative farming techniques, Tony and Meredith were developing new technology and management systems to handle stock individually instead of as a herd. They needed investment to commercialise the system that would allow Australian farmers to increase productivity and end-product quality.

This matters. People in the city forget where their food comes from. I want to share this.

As the night settled across the plains and I heard the occasional bird in the distance, millions of stars appeared. I gasped at the vast glitterscape as the three of us drove across the paddocks the following evening to have a campfire and dinner by the creek.

I had no idea. I've always loved astronomy but I had no idea what I was missing out on; how many stars I couldn't see when I've looked up before. This is desert magic. I could stay here and gaze beyond the Milky Way forever.

The Outback night made me impossibly small and the vastness was a relief. I felt a homecoming. Star song in my bones.

Days later, in Brisbane again, I felt the tangle of congestion and noise more keenly. For months, as I walked through the city or washed the dishes or tried to find a car park amid the clamour, I craved quiet and open space. Joni Mitchell had once sung the line that danced in my mind: "I am porous with travel fever."

Wrapped in a pervasive temporariness, I was *willing* to leave at any moment but I wasn't able. I tried to bury the agitation as I continued to work. I wrote and got paid; I wrote and was ignored — pitching into the 'freelancers' abyss' of no reply.

One wish was answered: the drought broke in Bourke for Christmas 2009.

But then it flooded.

36

One February day in Brisbane I turned 32. It was 2010. That night, in the quiet, I lay on my back on my couch holding the orange hardcover edition of *The Daring Book For Girls*, in smiling disbelief that a friend I hadn't seen since *primary school* had come to my birthday and gifted it to me.

*People came. In the rain. I **do** have friends; good people. I'm lucky.*

Everyone seemed to enjoy the game, too.

I had handed a small sheet of paper to each of the dozen or so guests as they arrived alone or in pairs at Brisbane's Powerhouse. It listed 'find people who...' tasks. Things like, 'Find people who: are planning to walk for charity; have thrown coins in the Trevi Fountain; can explain the acronym LARP; can hum the Degrassi Junior High theme song; know where the Wombles live; were born overseas; can tell you how old Doctor Who is...'

My golden impression of the party was thrown off days later though, when Samantha told me something like, "People mentioned things they'd spoken about or done with you and I had no idea what they were talking about. It's like you're a different person with everyone you meet."

Perhaps she was right. Or maybe I inadvertently found others who reflected different parts of my personality.

Aren't we all chameleons in some way?

———

That year became a voracious limbo. Full and empty. Sweet and stale. Beautiful, with hard edges. I often woke at 3am with the world in my head and the sleeping city beyond my balcony — and couldn't shake the sense of sifting, sorting and gathering.

Some sort of preparation.

I worked part time, on purpose.

I discovered Kerouac, by accident.

Under the lemon tree, on the strip of lawn near the clotheslines at the back of my apartment block, I devoured *On the Road*. Mum and I took a quick trip to Far North Queensland. I began to wonder what it was like in San Francisco.

On cold Saturdays, I'd bake pumpkin while boiling potato and onion in chicken stock, then blend it all together with sloshes of coconut milk. Sometimes I'd wish there was someone with whom I could share it. I'd wish there was someone who'd come in and smell the care and garlic entwined and know they were home. But then I'd indulge in the solo-only act of wiping my bowl clean with my finger — and ladle more into the bowl.

Amid a cloying sameness, I tried to illuminate my way with others' wisdom.

Some days, I sat on the kitchen bench by the sink with my legs bunched to my chest, like a cat curling into the warmest, highest patch of sunlight. I often looked across the suburbs as I listened to ABC radio: mornings slipped away with *Life Matters*, *Books and Arts* and *The Conversation Hour*; or *By Design* and *The*

Science Show. A little punch-drunk on new facts and stories, I'd reel and reflect as my head rested against the doors of the over-counter cupboards.

What can I take from that? How does it apply to me?

I poured Alain de Botton's *The Pleasures and Sorrows of Work* into me like a parched woman hallucinating in the desert. Hugh McLeod's cartoons on creativity roused me.

One night, in a lavender-scented bubble bath, I lay reading Barbara Sher's *Refuse to Choose* (a follow up to *I Could Do Anything, If Only I Knew What it Was*) and the pages blurred as I cried with relief. She saw into every taste-the-world pore of me; each quiet longing and wisp of boldness that didn't have a name. She championed multi-passionate people — 'Scanners' as she'd named them; us — who loved variety and thrived on learning and seeking new experiences.

Barbara knew, *just knew*, my thrill at understanding strands of disparate topics and weaving them into an everyday tapestry. Upon it I could wonder at all life was — and importantly, what it could be — to configure the next step towards my sense of a better place. Even when it was just dreaming in the dark.

In that bath, cold, with bubbles dissolved, I understood: to recognise who we are, sometimes we need to see the pieces assembled elsewhere. I'd found a reprieve from being buoyed but wearied by my intense curiosity, my wanderlust, my short attention span.

That's what Scanners do. It's not just me!

While books and radio gave me invaluable insight, they couldn't keep me from all that had to be lived.

———

Nana was in hospital. I don't remember exactly when, but her room had a large window and a sweeping view across the

Brisbane suburbs — the city centre's pocket of skyscrapers, in the distance.

A metal trolley clanked in the hallway. An attendant brought lunch in and I helped Nana sit up. I wasn't quite sure how to do it.

"Not easy with a new hip, eh?" I said, grabbing another pillow to put behind her.

"I'll be right, sweet," Nana said, looking frail as she tried to adjust her position in bed.

She'd always been beautifully made up; many of her clothes hand-made and a riot of colour. It was the first time I fed her. By the end of lunch, she looked a little sprightlier.

"We were a bit worried about you," I said. "You've been in the wars recently."

"Oh, don't worry, sweetheart. You can't kill me with an axe!"

We both laughed. It was a horrifying image but my mind snapped back to the sentiment.

"That's right! You're a trooper, aren't you?"

She was ready for more sleep.

When Nana was home, for a while I stopped in more frequently to see her. One day I visited when she was alone at home because Pop was in hospital having *his* hip replaced. She struggled a little to make our cups of tea. I can't explain why I didn't think more of it. She was having trouble remembering what was where.

But that day was one of the first times since I was a child that just the two of us talked. I laughed. A lot.

Nana is hilarious. How did I not know this?

I realised that on birthdays, Christmases and at any other visiting time, Pop had always been there — and he dominated the conversation. He would often cut Nana off when she spoke. It drove me crazy but I rarely said anything beyond, "What was it you were saying, Nana?"

She loved my new little blue car and I remember her standing at the edge of the driveway, waving me off in it, hand held high after blowing me a kiss.

My phone rang hours later at home.

"Darling, where did you go?" Nana asked.

"What do you mean?" I said.

"Well, one minute we were talking in the lounge room, and the next you were just gone," she said. "I didn't know where you went."

"We were talking but then I came home — you waved me off in my car, remember?"

"Oh. I must have lost some time. I don't remember that at all. Are you sure?"

"Yes, I'm sure. I'm okay. There's nothing to worry about here. Are you feeling all right now?"

"Good, good. I wanted to see where you were. They say...they say there's something happening to my brain."

My heart lurched.

"I'm sure it's just a small thing, Nana. Try not to worry about it. I'm sure you're going to be fine," I lied.

I hung up and cried for a long time.

———

Kate was the only person I knew who read novels while walking down the street. An ex-journalist with a quick wit and dry laugh, we'd bonded four years earlier over Doctor Who and Astro Boy, while I managed a media account for her employer. She'd made me promise not to apologise when my company invariably made mistakes.

"I've got a mate you should meet," Kate said.

"Oh yeah? Who's that then?" I asked.

It's not like I'm meeting anyone any other way. It's been three years since Cardiac Guy. At least with a set-up, the bloke's not an unknown quantity.

He was a FIFO guy — fly in/fly out — who worked in the mines overseas and was intermittently back in Australia. Kate had known him since uni through a friend they had in common. She ensured he and I were invited to a birthday party for one of her kids.

By the time the sun got closer to the horizon, I'd eaten my fill of fairy bread and drunk a lot of lemonade. Late-afternoon rays peeped through the trees next to Kate's small front yard and there were only a few 'hangers on' left, drinks in hand, stay-at-home parents enjoying adult conversation.

Mr FIFO and I had only said a few words to each other.

There's an old soul in that body of his. Hmmm, in that capable, muscular body.

"He's got a heart of gold," Kate said, leaning close to my ear, when she caught a glance between the two of us.

"And soon he's going to fly away," I said.

"Yes, but think of how good it will be when he's *here*. Want me to give him your phone number?"

"Nah. I'll go and talk to him."

It would be many more months until he and I were in the same place again.

37

'Frisco, 'Cisco, San Fran, SF. You rolled off my tongue but stuck to my brain.

I chalked the crudest of histories as I walked you: gold rush, earthquake, Harvey Milk, dot com. That didn't do you justice but I saw at a glance you were a golden gate to a whole other kind of city that kissed the Pacific. A topographic and cultural feast.

Topped and tailed, you were Alcatraz to Zen. Your spring wind was a razor; your fog a wonderland veil. I hiked your metropolitan hills; I cursed my inappropriate shoes.

In *Tales of the City* you reflected yourself from the stage and I sat next to a stranger. Within the ricochet of intermission, my cabaret-singer seat mate flew me to his world, and in the nose-bleed seats of the theatre, we never got up to stretch and the lights went down again.

I could have died happy at City Lights Bookstore.

At the Embarcadero, once a sea wall fronting a harbour, you revealed a little more: San Francisco sits on the bones of ships.

My coordinates were askew. Burying my face in the darkness under a down-filled quilt didn't help. When I studied the old painted ceiling with an intensity I'd forgotten I could muster, still nothing happened. From my third-floor, courtyard-facing room, I heard silence roar through the monastery. The deepest pre-dawn sleep was spun around that 1920s slice of city. The kind of sleep that curls through those who will wake and meditate in a couple of hours.

Springtime San Francisco was at my window. I was 33. It was 2011.

I got up and put on my coat, padded past my ensuite and into the kitchenette. I scooped my shoes — set by the door, not to be worn inside the room — onto bed-socked feet. Silently descending four flights of grand staircase, I felt I was on some kind of midnight boarding school break out.

But I wasn't about to walk the streets on my own in the small hours. I sought something else.

When I entered the dark, boiler-warmed communal kitchen, disorientation stuck. My recollection of the layout, and likely light switch locations, was fuzzy at best. It was my first night there. In the kitchen, heat seeped pleasantly onto my skin and I realised how cold the rest of the building was.

I peered at my surrounds and adjusted to the half-light. The tea was waiting, in substantial glass jars with white screw-top lids, just through another doorway. Finding the *green* tea was a trick of memory and I'd carefully noted where the clean mugs and glasses could be found.

Turning to add hot water, I caught a scream in the back of my throat. Someone was immediately behind me.

"Sorry to scare you," he whispered. "So, you couldn't sleep either?"

"Oh wow, you did scare me! Man. No rest for the wicked or the jet lagged," I said.

I was thankful I'd not actually screamed, and that my usual response to shock had not passed my lips. He set about making tea too, after illuminating the tiny kitchen for residents only, tucked to the side of the main food preparation area. We were two of about 70 tucked up in the Zen Center, a world within a world. We sat opposite each other at a round table, at 3am. Unsure of the etiquette, I sipped and said nothing.

Five months earlier, in January, a violent flood had bloated Brisbane — and most of Queensland. People, animals and houses gone. I'd cried at successive evening news bulletins, for the loss *and* the rally, the heart.

We all want to help; we just need to know how.

Afterwards, I'd dragged my dead-weight inertia to the office for months. The office: climate controlled; conduct controlled. An atmosphere of headaches. I was aware of better ways to spend my time but not any that would fill my bank account. I was working full time again.

Spent and grasping for something to reinvigorate me, I'd noted for a couple of months what and for whom I was grateful. I saw my parents in a different light: retrospectively more appreciative each year that they'd been there for me to come home to again after Normandy, even as their world crumbled; that they were still there in their own ways. A renewed appreciation for clean sheets and hot water and old friends and cloudless days came to the fore, too. But it didn't sate me in the way I'd wanted.

How can such simple things be enough?

I was sure only a plane ticket and a travel writing gig would be enough.

Wrapped in the kindly presence of the stranger, I felt a silent invitation to talk, if I wished. I told him a little of what I'd felt recently and that I'd hoped I'd find something to reset my mind there at the Zen Center, in that nook of a city I had been thinking about for a while.

"Ah, Buddha has called you," he said softly.

I couldn't say I was also there because I was intrigued. Because I thought it would make a quirky story. Because it was the only place I could afford to stay, considering I'd decided to treat myself and book the swanky Westin downtown in a few days, during a big travel conference I was going to, before heading north — and the whole shebang was on my dime.

But who knows? Maybe Buddha did call me. I don't know anymore.

We spoke easily, quietly. He was calm and calming. The beguiling atmosphere of the refuge began its spell.

There might really be something beautiful here.

Content and drowsy and thankful, I returned to my room. Cocooning myself in the quilt again, my soul soared as my eyes closed. Just as the meditation gong pulled everyone from sleep. I didn't move for another five hours.

————

The best way into it was with a massage first, I figured. The massage unknotted my travel-weary muscles but it didn't really prepare me mentally. Of course, it couldn't. I was delaying the moment.

Delaying the second I abandoned my towel and walked naked, under the gaze of a room full of women, across the tiles — the dim warm air soft on my skin — before lowering myself as unselfconsciously as I could into the spa.

Yes, this is me. All of me. How do I strike the balance between confident and relaxed? I'm sure there's a trick of posture that helps.

No one was actually watching.

I was trying not to look anywhere. But I was curious.

Curious in the way photographers and artists are about shape and the fall of shadows, how our eyes render depth, how light gives form its visible texture. Curious in the way poets are about liberty and shame and unmasking. Curious in the way anthropologists are about social history and ritual.

I'd never been anywhere that allowed me to witness the female form in its grand and nuanced variety. The only other woman I'd seen naked was my mum.

*If we all saw more of this, there'd be less angst in the world. If we all **felt** more of this — what it looks like these women are feeling... what is it? nonchalance? acceptance? contentment? — whole industries would topple.*

Too much thinking, Sara.

I closed my eyes. I felt the water. I let my arms float in front of me as I sat on the submerged ledge.

Hush. Let go.

I heard water flowing. I felt the rhythm of collective breath. I inhaled deeply — some fresh concoction only just detectable, like cucumber and mint leaves — and relaxed as I expelled all my breath.

I am here.

Breathe in.

I am here.

Breathe out.

I am.

Breathe in.

I am.

...

———

Despite my intentions, I never made it to the 5am meditation at the San Francisco Zen Center. I was jet-lagged for four days and my adventuring had begun around noon each day. But I went mid-morning, at the end of my stay, when there was an introductory session open to the public.

A monk with a soft German accent and unlined face had a presence that *almost* made me believe in auras. About 25 of us perched cross-legged at the edge of cushions, wriggling to find a balance between a straight back, relaxed shoulders and a posture that enabled sitting still for more than 30 seconds. The monk spoke about the traditions, customs and terminology associated with the Center's meditation practice. How to walk into the *dojo*, how to sit; the format of a session.

"But," came the first word from the crowd when he opened the floor to questions, "why should we meditate?"

The conversation continued something like:

"This isn't about being prescriptive. It's something each of us, if we feel called, can experience on our own terms," the monk said.

"Um, I guess I mean what do you get out of it? Not just you personally — anyone?"

The monk was a little perplexed.

"Well, the practice is the benefit."

"Okay, doing it is good but what is it about the practice that is meaningful?"

"Sometimes there's no meaning beyond the experience itself," the monk said, appearing to grapple with why this wasn't just obvious to us.

I don't remember how, but I know I re-phrased the question in yet another way for him.

"Ah. Well. Meditation helps us become more ourselves," he said, a relieved smile just disappearing as a bell indicated it was time for us all to sit in silence.

After the session, I climbed the grand staircase again for the final time, to collect my luggage from my sun-doused room. In that elevated space, there was a shining moment, where the accumulated peace and welcome of the preceding days and silent nights let me touch the calm. The stillness found beneath the warfare of my enemy-twins: wanderlust and anxiety.

———

I ate some sky and hit the road in Idaho.

Swooping onto Interstate 84 from Boise, I cut across a rain-smudged prairie, hemmed by distant mountains. I turned east onto Highway 20 and began to climb. Tenacious snow topped a peak ahead, shining silver in a pocket of sun — in June.

I'll stop at the next town. I'm starving.

Fairfield had to do. Its few dozen houses and handful of streets were huddled in the sweep of a great southern prairie. Its café was all Formica, linoleum and another era. It was the kind of place ranchers drove 100 kilometres (60 miles) to with an empty coffee mug, looking for lunch and respite from sharp-cold air.

One of the older men in the small group that had just arrived caught me watching.

He's spotted the stranger in town.

He raised his cream-coloured hat as he approached, splintering from the group who sat at another of the three tables. After his opening line, he said: "Do you mind if I sit here, ma'am?"

"Not at all — go right ahead."

We got to talking.

"There are two ways to cook 'em," he said, "you throw them in the branding fire and they pop, or you deep fry 'em."

"What *do* bull's testicles taste like?"

"Well," he said, blue eyes flashing and grey moustache stretching above a grin, "not like chicken".

He obligingly answered all the questions I laid between us on the plastic table. I was a kid in a candy store. His manner was easy. Time on the land filled a chunk of afternoon; the seasons were hard and didn't suffer fools.

This guy would get along well with Tony out in Bourke.

My toasted cheese sandwich dripped oil as he talked. I ate it just to get it out of sight. The café food was basic but that distillation of life was intoxicating.

"So, where are you going?" he asked.

"I'm looping in and out of Boise on a 9-day trip — to Sun Valley, the Sawtooth Mountains, Stanley and McCall."

He whistled. "Hitting all the high spots, eh? You'll have to come back and see the *real* Idaho."

Don't tempt me.

As I climbed up into my red beast of an SUV again, high on whatever it was that made me thrum to my core, I thought: *This is where I am most myself: drinking in others' stories and pushing on to the horizon. The big sky blooming above.*

Beyond Sun Valley, from Galena Summit on Highway 75, I marvelled at the clear view to the Stanley Basin and Sawtooth Mountains — and that on the way, I'd squeezed my vehicle past a group of cyclists.

Who's up for a 2,600-metre (8530-foot) climb before lunch?

The Basin cradled ghost towns; riches and desolation were unearthed in unequal measure for those who sought silver and gold there 150 years earlier. I'd read that more than 50 of the Sawtooth's 147 peaks pushed beyond 3,048 metres (10,000 feet) and their granite protrusions held more than 300 lakes.

A postage-stamp of a town by the Salmon River, Stanley felt like an old Western set. Dusty streets with names like 'Ace of Diamonds' flanked wooden cabins and only about 60 people were year-round residents. I was in town for one night.

I walked up a ridge above the handful of houses and

watched the Sawtooths' silhouette etch into the twilight. A great sky-kissing curtain of silence pulled across the high country and I let it settle upon me. The day slipped away. A tiny patch of illuminated windows glowed in an expanse that, as I watched, was wholly swallowed by night.

My breath, and the occasional bird, were the only sounds. I found comfort in the sturdiness of the rock under my feet. The great gape of geological time was so large, it made moments precious.

This time will never come again.

I was a wisp in a majestic universe.

Later, alone and cool to the touch in my motel room, I fell asleep to the sound of the couple next door making love.

38

The connection between Brisbane and Indonesia wasn't great but Mr FIFO and I persisted. It was the first time we'd been able to talk to each other in weeks. Kate seemed so pleased at her eventual match.

"...and you wouldn't believe it, I was in a tiny town in the middle of nowhere in Idaho, and a group of farmers came in—"

"Hang on, what was that last bit?"

"After the travel conference in San Francisco I went to Sonoma for a few days — it was beautiful — then up to Oregon, then Boise, in Idaho. Can you hear me?"

"Yeah, that's better now, keep going."

"Anyway, one of the farmers came over to my table — in Idaho that is — and he actually said, 'You're not from 'round these parts, are you?' It was priceless!...Hello?"

"....Good one. Hey, I have to go. I'm glad you had a good time. You sound really happy."

"I am. Oh, okay, well when you find out, let me know how long you'll be back for next time. Let's hope it's three weeks; one is far too short!"

"I will."

"'Bye! I miss you."

"Miss you too."

Once when he'd flown out, he'd texted me on the way to the airport:

 I finally know what it's like to go when I don't want to leave someone.

———

Anticipation hit and shimmied in my innards as I drove 25 minutes across Brisbane to Mr FIFO's place. I skirted the city on the Riverside Expressway; then stop-started at the traffic lights en route to, and past, the shopping centre at Indooroopilly ("Indro" to all the locals). My 'butterflies' always peaked as I climbed the bends of his tree-lined street. The driveway was just beyond a blind corner.

His house was an old, sprawling multi-level affair, including a musty basement converted to a studio apartment with an office. The office made me recoil; I couldn't shake the sensation something bad had happened there. A rambling garden-to-be terraced down the steep block at the back. A large in-ground swimming pool sat at the bottom of the yard, covered for half the year.

Each time I arrived, I'd follow the sound of power tools or look for extension cords or check what kind of new building supplies sat on the front veranda.

"Hello?!"

He was always in the middle of something.

When the rain came and it got dark in the middle of the afternoon, we'd turn on all the house lights so we could see where we were painting, or he was sanding, or I was holding something level so he could mark up the drill holes. Other wet days we'd just down tools and sit in folding camp chairs with cups of tea out the back. We listened to the birds and breathed in the smell of damp soil and dripping leaves, and talked about what the house would be like when the renovation was done. It was slow work.

His time at home varied. 'Home' was my description. He said he didn't really have one.

We shopped for a king-sized bed when our bedroom at his place was finished, but sometimes the best sex was just up against the wall in the hallway. At the edge of abandon. I suspected there was so much I'd never quite felt and he was calling me over the cliff. Even when he was angry at the world and that made me afraid; even when I could see his heartbreak and that made me sad, I needed his lithe body against me, inside me. His masculinity had a hard veneer and it called forth *my* power.

The power and comfort I needed.

Anxiety had begun to snap at my heels again. At work, at home, with him. It spat venom into my ear — just below my consciousness because I couldn't tell you what it said — and it shook me in my dreams and made life feel unstable. As if everywhere had become a set of theatre props that could be rearranged at any time.

But in a handful of moments, he and I locked animal eyes. We were fierce and scratching. I was liberated and wanted to tear down the world.

———

Mr FIFO and I sat opposite each other, chatting at the wooden table on his front veranda. He blindsided me in a conversation mostly forgotten, except:

"People who travel a lot are always running away from something."

"I've never been running away from anything," I said. "No, absolutely not."

"Yeah? What have you been doing it for then?"

"I've been…running *towards* things. Running *into* the world. I'm curious."

He shook his head as he shifted in his seat, putting his paint speckled hands on his hips; his dirty work pants hidden from view.

"Nah, not buying it."

"I don't care if you 'buy' it or not."

How can you know so much about me and understand so little? What about you, Mr **Fly in/Fly out**?

————

I probably looked like a power walker, but I didn't waste energy punching the air with bent arm swings. I'd plied the same suburban streets near my place about nine months earlier during the flood, when Brisbane's spilled and spreading river swept mercilessly and debris-ridden towards Moreton Bay.

Now the water was a broad slick of grey-brown, unreflective, under a sky that had begun to smudge with cloud. A 'for sale' sign hammered firmly into a manicured lawn read 'Millionaire's Row at an Affordable Price'. Only metres away, a crow swooped to haul a complete rat carcass from the ground into the branches of a flowering tree.

Stilling myself closer to the bank and the ferry stop, the former wool stores on the opposite bank caught my eye, their handsome red brick enduring. Their windows would have once reflected heady trading days. I watched as a barge, kayak and ferry appeared, keeping their own quiet rhythm.

I needed to move again.

The light turned apricot; the sun a disc behind a brewing storm. The sky began to break, and the first raindrops cracked onto dead leaves resting on roadside clover. I turned home. No solace by the river that day; my internal jangling unabated. I climbed the hill of my street, just a bit higher into electric air as the thunder began in earnest.

———

My relationship seemed to be its own entity. There was me, him and it. We were contortionists.

We strayed into another conversation about property. It started innocuously but soon we were snared in verbal combat again.

"You say you really want to buy a house, but everything you've done and all you're doing — *all your actions* — are contrary to that," he said.

I couldn't concede the sting. He owned three houses. I couldn't concede the sting of that either.

Sometime later, my volley: "I'm not going to apologise for wanting to travel; for wanting a 'big' life. I'm not broken. I'm not something to be fixed. Why do you keep acting like I need fixing?"

"I know, I know. I do act like that and I don't know why," he replied.

"I'm not asking you for money, I'm not asking you for anything. Except that you accept me for who I am."

The volatility passed.

We talked. *Really* talked. He'd felt screwed over and screwed shut for so long. He'd let me in as far as he could; as far as he'd ever done.

I told him about my anxiety. It was still hard to talk about and only a handful of people knew.

"Is there anything that would help?" he said.

I realised I hadn't been breathing properly; I exhaled fully after my short, shallow breaths and staccato sentences.

"Well, it would be really great if you could come to The Counsellor with me — I check in with her a few times a year — and you could hear from her about what's going on, you know, so you understand more about what I'm feeling, what anxiety is—"

"Oh, I'm not going near any counsellor."

"But you just asked what you could do to help. That would really help."

"No, I didn't say *I* was going to do anything. *I* don't want to do anything. I meant what can *you* do that would help."

And there it was, twisted into a jagged-edged thing.

———

He was back in town and sounded strange on the phone.

"I need to see you," Mr FIFO said.

"Want to start Christmas early, eh? I'll be there soon," I said.

"No, it's better if I come there. Can I come over?"

"Oh, okay. Is everything all right?"

I'd been due at his house in a few hours to celebrate — not just because it was Christmas Eve but the other thing: he'd left his job in Indonesia to come back to Brisbane. For a fresh start in one place. We were going to make the future we kept talking about. The one we'd find once we got through "all this *stuff*".

He'd be at my apartment in 25 minutes.

As I looked out to the city in the summer heat, in the silence after his call, I shuddered. And amid the welling upset, the fire shot of adrenaline and the wasting, empty-stomach sense of the break up about to happen, I felt something else. Something foreign.

I tried to find its edges first, as though I was blindfolded in some awful party game. But it blew the blindfold away and rose strong and calm from some deep-drop place inside me. It was a voice that spoke softly but filled the whole room. I was sad. It was not.

If you cannot see the value in me, I will not explain it to you. Go if you cannot see it.

Oh.

In that instant I was back in Normandy, boxes and bags packed and en route to London, desperate for my husband to ask me to stay.

39

"The thing is," I said to The Counsellor, "after we broke up — I just sat with it."

"Hmmm?" she said, head nodding.

I took off my jacket; her new office was invitingly warm. Autumn was in its death throes.

I was 34. It was 2012.

"Well, after we broke up the *second* time — I *never* go back and I *hate* that I broke that rule — anyway, I sat with the bloody 'break up feeling' and sat with it some more. I felt all of it. I didn't distract myself with anything or anyone. I planted myself in each moment and felt the anger and pain and sadness from everything."

"Good."

"Then I tried to find the lessons."

I'd written lists and stared into space and thought and read and followed trails through the blogosphere and christened new notebooks and had long phone conversations and cups of tea with friends. Then I stared out the window some more.

What are my values?

What matters to me?

When am I at my best?

Who makes me feel good and why?

Where are the patterns in my life that don't help me? (What am I doing and what do I allow others to do?)

How do I need to change?

"Excellent."

"But after a while, all that sitting and feeling. It just got boring. I mean, *really* boring. What's the point of that?"

"Boring, eh?" she nodded a couple of times slowly, exaggeratedly, with her eyebrows raised and said, "Well there you go."

"Oh, it's a process, right? Follow it to its natural end and that's how you're ready to move beyond it?"

She just let my question hang in the air. I continued.

"Okay, well, another thing: I think I'm going to have to find another job. Again."

"You know how to do that."

"Yeah. Five government communications roles in five years. But I've only just found something I *really* like."

"What's that?"

"It's called user experience design. I didn't even know it was a 'thing', but it is and it's fascinating."

"What does that involve?"

"Well, at the moment I'm working on a redevelopment of a website, intranet site and an intranet portal. And the user experience — 'UX' for short — design process is all about doing research and testing, and following design principles, to make the site effective for the person using it. Rather than the site just reflecting a department or company structure. That sort of thing. I'm not explaining it very well but there's a whole field dedicated to it."

"Okay, but why do you need a new job?"

"Oh, yeah, it looks like there's going to be a state election soon and after that no government contracts will be renewed or extended. I'm on contract; I've never had a permanent position. There's no role for me to return to."

"But isn't that because you never wanted a permanent position?"

"Yes. True. I guess I've been lucky — the longest it's taken me to find a new job since I started in government in '07 has been two months."

"Is there any reason that's likely to change?"

"I guess not. But you never know, do you?"

————

"Here's your desk," said my new boss, pointing to the one next to his as morning winter sunshine was striking holes in the clouds and I was already missing the sleep-ins of the previous six weeks. I put my bag on the seat that looked like it didn't adjust properly.

"This is the rest of the content team," he said, indicating towards a few other people nearby who looked up and waved hello, returning to their screens after a few words of greeting.

"Okay, so, tell me about your publication process — where's your style guide kept?" I asked.

"Style guide?" he looked puzzled.

"You know, the document that ensures content consistency. The reference describing appropriate language, tone, abbreviations...?"

"We don't have one."

"Oh, okay. Well, who approves content before it's live on the Web?"

"No one."

"No one?"

"There's no crazy bureaucracy here — you write it and hit publish."

That explains a lot.

"Right, well I'm happy to create a style guide," I said.

"We've made it this far without one," he countered.

We toured the floor.

At least the office is modern with a lot of natural light... I can catch the ferry to work... The UX team is next to the content team so that could be handy...

Finally, he said: "And here's the kitchen — where we all finish early for drinks on Friday."

"Ah. That's a lovely idea, but I have to be honest and let you know I don't drink."

"It's a team bonding thing."

"Sure, but drinking isn't *my* thing."

The head of the division I was in was always spoken of in deferential tones. I wondered what he looked like; how his demeanour conveyed the power and influence he obviously had. The first time I saw him was a few weeks into the job. He was sitting in a wheelbarrow, being wheeled about the office by my boss, raising an open bottle of beer — that I suspected wasn't his first — yelling, "Drinks are about to start!"

Kill me now.

———

In the early hours of a spring morning, after my alarm had scratched into my unwilling consciousness again, I sent a desperate email. It was an application to a 12-week business development course online for 'Scanner', free-thinking types. For those caught in, and frustrated by, the corporate world. For

those passionate about escaping the 9–5 and living on their
own terms.

———

"Now, let me get this straight," The Counsellor said. She went on
to say something like: "You're working full time, in a new job
with a boss who's — shall we say — unhelpful; you're preparing
to start a business on the side; you're concerned about your
grandparents and you're visiting your nana, who has dementia
and is in a care home, on the weekends."

"Yes," I said.

"Now, this is your dad's mum — but your dad lives with his
long-term girlfriend more than three hours away now, and
your mum isn't in the picture because your parents are
divorced."

"Yes."

"And your dad comes down as often as he can, but your
brother doesn't help with your nana, so the only people nearby
all the time are you and your great aunt?" she asked.

"Yes, that's about it in a nutshell."

"And you want to know how you can be more resilient?"

"Yes. I'm finding this really hard right now."

"I would suggest you *already are* resilient. Listen to the
scenario I just outlined. *Of course* you're going to feel stressed —
that's normal," she said. "This is a very difficult time."

"So what do I do?"

"Keep doing what you've been trying to do: eat well, sleep as
best you can. Be kind to yourself."

"Really? There's no other strategy or tip or book I could read
right now?"

"When we first met — what was it? four years ago? — you
didn't think you could get on a plane to go to a friend's wedding.

Look how far you've come. You're much stronger than
you think."

———

I found a confidant at work. Her eyes had widened with glee as I
told her about the online course I was doing that would help me
create my own business. I raved about the instructor, my
classmates and the premise of making a living in a way that
harnessed natural strengths and talents. How showing
personality in business was not only okay, but essential.

"Oh, meant to tell you too, I spoke to Dave in Sydney again
last night," I said.

"Remind me...?" she asked, eyebrows raised but brow
knotted in an I-should-have-remembered-this way.

"He's the only one in the course in the same time zone as me.
Remember, almost everyone else is in the UK; well, Dave's from
the UK, Newcastle — crazy accent — but he lives here now."

"Okay..."

"...and we had to buddy up to do one of the course exercises.
So we swapped details, did the exercise, and we've kept
in touch."

"Yes! Got it. I remember now. Ooooh, is anything going on
there? How often do you talk?"

"God no, I've been through enough for a while! He's in
Sydney anyway. No, he's just a really nice guy. We talk about all
sorts of stuff — about life, travel, the kind of businesses we want
to make — probably about once a week for around an hour."

"Wow. A guy who doesn't mind talking on the phone."

"I know. It's so refreshing to talk to someone for the sake of
the conversation. There's no deciding what to wear; he's not
perving on my cleavage. We don't mention work. I have no idea
what he does."

"Speaking of work, better get back to it. Ugh. Keep me posted!"

"I will!"

At lunch, I'd often dash to the closest green space, craving quiet. I had to make do with a wedge of ground that basically formed a large traffic island. But I could sit under trees, on the grass, and with a little difficulty ignore the noise. I checked my email there one hot November day to find a note from Dave that said 'This is what I told you about' and a link.

The link was the teaser trailer for a conference-type-thing in Portland, Oregon. Something called the World Domination Summit or 'WDS' for short. I was enthralled and played the video twice. The event was staunchly independent — no sponsors, no sales pitches — and the WDS ethos seemed to revolve around community, adventure and service.

It doesn't look like a cult.

But they never do, do they?

I was pretty sure it was secular. Dave had attended several months earlier and already had his ticket for the following July.

"Is it a conference for despots and dictators?" Mum joked when I first mentioned it.

———

One evening in early December I sat at my dining table with an empty stomach, my face a white-blue wash in the glow of my laptop screen. I could hear my heartbeat roaring when I hadn't moved. Perspiration dripped into my T-shirt. I held my breath as I hit 'Publish' in the backend of my website and launched a kernel of my dream into cyberspace. A potential exit pod to take me away from the mad bad bosses of the world.

*I don't care what happens in that little job anymore. I have this! This site I've **made**. This space: a home for restless multi-passionate* *people; a champion of embracing the explorer within to find the best version of a self. I'll fill it with books I'll write, and stories of wonderful people, and who-knows-what-else! I don't **really** know what you'll become yet, We are the Treasure Hunters — what sort of business you'll be — but god I love this feeling.*

Three weeks later I quit my job. I had contract work for January.

I've been getting contracts for five years — I'll be fine.

40

On my drives to and from visiting Nana, I'd been turning up the radio far louder than I usually would, getting 35 minutes of bass under my skin as I auto-piloted along Old Cleveland Road. I imagined secret London raves and sprawling, Hollywood high life parties.

Sweat, dance, dance. Put your hands in the air!

It had been too long since I danced up a storm. There were many things on my 'too long since...' list. There was a whole other person within me, who I thought had left long ago. But she was still there and she wanted a headiness seared into her bloodstream again.

I ripped up the road home at night, wanting speed and sex and some kind of bacchanalian exit point from it all.

Pop died.

I sobbed on my kitchen floor as I unpacked food from what had once been Nana and Pop's pantry into my own; Dad had said there was no point it going to waste, and did I want any furniture?

My brother married in Cleveland, by the lighthouse, as black clouds gathered. Adam looked really happy. An ex-tropical

cyclone was on its way. For two days after the reception, gale-
force winds smashed South East Queensland.

All that, before the end of January.

———

Conversation between the three of us at my 35th birthday dinner
at a waterfront restaurant in Cleveland was surprisingly easy. I
asked the waiter to take a photo because I didn't know if or
when we'd all be together again. Mum scoffed — but she never
liked photos of herself. Dad wasn't a great fan of having his
photo taken either. But I treasured the blurry shot on my phone.
We were all smiling, remarkably.

Several Saturdays after my birthday, I woke to the news via
voicemail that Nana had had a stroke the night before. She was
'holding on at the moment'. The message had been left eight
hours earlier. I called Dad, my hands clammy and anxiety
billowing.

He didn't answer.

Shit.

I called Adam. "Is she still with us? Have I missed her?" The
tremor caught my tongue at the end of 'missed' so the 'her' was
breathy and only half spoken.

Nana's hospital bed had moved rooms four times in the
preceding two weeks, without any communication to the family:
to the nurses' station for high priority care; further away from it
when the medical opinion was there was nothing left to be
done, other than 'maintain comfort'. I had arrived to an empty
bed twice in that period. My stomach flipped each time and the
world spiralled in those brief seconds before I found someone to
ask where she was.

Now, she lay motionless in bed with the blanket pulled up
under her neck. As if she were already gone. I briefly panicked she

may have, and no one had realised. The light in the room was milky; the walls an insipid beige. The beige felt like some sort of betrayal.

*Where is the colour? She **needs** colour.*

I sat by her bed and held her hand.

"Nana, it's me, it's Sara. I'm here. I don't know if you can hear me but I'm going to talk to you anyway. You're not on your own. Remember how I used to love looking through your jewellery box when I was little? You had all those rings you used to wear; I was fascinated by them. And remember how we used to make cakes, before Mum and Dad moved to the farm? I was about four and you told me it was very important to make a small 'dam' in the flour to hold the eggs and milk. One year I helped you make the Christmas cake and it was *so* hard to stir, I had no idea the mixture would be that heavy! It was delicious though. I miss your Christmas cakes. Sorry, that's not what you want to be hearing about right now," I said.

There was no drip anymore. She couldn't swallow. The chart at the end of her bed said 'Nil by mouth'.

Sometimes, when you think death is in the same room, you find more love than you ever realised you had.

"Oh, and what about that photo you've had on the wall for so long, when Adam caught his first fish — remember? — you always said how proud he looked, and he was only about six," I added.

I stroked her hair. She began to stir.

I played a few classical music tracks from my phone.

She opened her eyes; it was a struggle because she'd been sedated. She opened her eyes and recognised me. And began to talk back. I leaned in close to hear her whispered words. She was frustrated by her compromised speech. She was exhausted. She was very, very thirsty. She rallied. Her tenacity floored me.

You're such a fighter.

Nana was discharged from hospital back to the care facility three days later.

Dave rang that evening but I didn't have the energy to take his call.

All the grief, fear, love and sheer gratitude for life became a dizzying and exhausting internal buzz. It allowed me to let everything fall away — and keep walking across the shifting ground.

We can only really feel our humanity when we allow ourselves to surrender; when we build our strength from the very vulnerability which threatens to crumple us.

————

The mid-autumn evening had a growing chill but Mum's house was snug. I looked down and traced my finger over the faint silky flower pattern on her fawn-coloured tablecloth. She sat opposite me with a few sheets of foolscap paper, jotting figures on it as we spoke. Dad sat on my left; he had a bundle of papers and files with him. He looked very tired.

I felt like the straight-A student suddenly sitting outside the headmaster's office.

"So, this is the amount outstanding once we subtract the flights and accommodation you've already paid for," Mum said, "but you'll have to make it two trips; coming home for a fortnight after Switzerland will save a lot."

"Yes, that makes sense," I said quietly.

"Any luck finding a flatmate so you're not paying full rent while you're away?" Mum asked, eyebrows raised with a small, hopeful smile.

"Oh, yes, my friend Ga—"

"Hang on just a minute," Dad cut me off. He looked at me:

"What do you think you're going to get out of all of this? What's the point?" He was worried.

My cheeks reddened. A pit of embarrassment caught in my throat — like food going down the wrong way — and a rock of shame hit my stomach.

Plans B and C had failed: I'd been unable to secure more contract work or a part-time job; my second business idea was still fledgeling, only making a tiny income. I was in new territory and almost at the end of my savings. I'd made commitments.

I never want to ask anyone for money again.

Be grateful you have parents to ask; parents who are in a position to help.

I never want to do this again.

In the way no one can ever quite explain without a nod to 'intuition', I knew I needed whatever was ahead, on other continents. But explaining that to an ex-military man was another thing altogether.

———

I tried to summon a fresh bout of courage and compassion each time I visited Nana at the live-in care facility. But I was small and afraid inside.

There was a dispenser of hand sanitiser by the locked front door that a nurse had to open for me. I applied the sanitiser thoroughly each time. The entry led to a large communal area that was half dining and half lounge. Each resident had a private room — with a comfy recliner by a window — and an ensuite.

*It's heartbreaking this is a **good** place to be. What about all the other elderly people who have nowhere to go when they can't look after themselves...?*

For a short time, Nana was lucid more frequently.

"I think it's wonderful; go and see the world while you can,"

Nana said. Looking into the communal courtyard from her room, she added, "When you get to my age, you only have memories to look back on...and you want to have something interesting to think about!"

We laughed.

"Exactly! I'm so glad you understand," I said.

I wish your son could see it the same way.

Something caught her attention; it may have been outside or 40 years ago. But she hadn't drifted as far as I thought.

"I never went overseas... Never left Australia."

"Where would you have gone if you could?"

"Oh! I don't know."

"Europe? America?"

"There are so many places to choose from, I wouldn't know where to start!"

"On my next trip, after London and Guernsey, I'm going to Switzerland. I've never been and it looks beautiful."

Her blue eyes flashed and she gave me a sly grin, "You might meet a banker! Wouldn't that be lovely?"

There she was: the enterprising woman who'd worked two jobs to ensure her son and daughter were well educated. The woman who forged a successful business despite the hardships her first marriage visited upon her.

"Sorry, what were we talking about, darl?"

I told her again that after Switzerland I was coming home for a couple of weeks, then going to America.

41

Brisbane, Australia
Monday, 6 May, 2013

*oes finalising accommodation really matter right now? I
don't think so. Shouldn't you be going?*
It was a still morning under steel-grey clouds and
that question had been circling for hours.

You should get going.

I can't.

I finally got to the care facility around 2pm.

"Is she still with us?" I asked as I found my great aunt in the
hallway near Nana's room.

"No, darling, she's not," she said.

"Oh. But..."

I should have come sooner.

"Your dad is just in with her now," she said as I
hugged her.

I estimated that Nana had died just as I'd left my apartment.
There are really only fragments in my memory from then: Dad,
coming out of Nana's room red faced and teary eyed. The two of

us hugging, "Dad, I'm so sorry." Me, tentatively going into the room as he went back in.

*I don't want to remember this. I don't want to remember her as a body. There's no description that prepares you for this; for seeing a person when the life is gone. No, I want to remember her as **her**. Not this.*

When the first stars came out that night, I saw them through my windscreen. I only heard the hush of the tide through the mangroves and onto the rocks because I'd let the driver's-side window down an inch. I wanted to push the steering wheel away from me, it was too claustrophobic, so I shifted the seat back, and looked into the disappearing light above the ocean. I still needed the car around me.

Twilight left and the darkness held fast. Dad was on his own at a pub somewhere — he'd declined company; I don't know where my brother and his wife were. I'd just left Mum's, Cleveland Point was only a five-minute drive away.

I always had a box of Kleenex in the car. I dug into it.

Here it is. This is where we were going, to the time you were actually gone. I know now why people don't say 'dead': it's too hard and final. I'm so sorry, Nana. I didn't know how to be in what was happening. I didn't talk to the doctors, I left that to Dad, like I was suddenly a kid and not a grown woman. As if I didn't have a right to find out for myself what was actually happening and why. Though I came to visit — and you woke up again after one of the strokes, remember? — I hid like a child when it looked like you'd been left to die; part of me thought that must have been right because you were in hospital. What the fuck? I'm so sorry.

*If we were doing this again — ha! that's ludicrous, and dear god, I wouldn't wish it upon anyone — I'd **be there**. And I'd be asking questions until I was satisfied with the answers.*

And when you asked when Pop was going to visit you, I didn't know how to tell you he'd died. And even when you'd asked before

that, I didn't know what to say because I still don't know what
happened between the two of you, before the hospital and the
care home.

  But the biggest sad thing: after all this life you've had, I still don't
really know you. We didn't work that way, our family, eh? I wish
you'd visited my place in Brisbane before all of this. Maybe you
wanted to? I know you'd have liked it.

I sobbed through a sludge of guilt. As I blew clotted gunk
into tissue after tissue, purging, I knew Nana wouldn't want me
to be thinking any of those things. Her life hadn't been hers
anymore and she deserved better.

She grew beautiful gardens, baked delicious cakes and could
sew anything.

When I got out into the night and walked by the water, I felt
newly exposed, as though a layer of protection had peeled away.
I felt a rising swell — my imagination conjuring what it might
be like to be an orphan. I felt the pull and drag of anxiety's
undercurrent but I would not go down. Even when a fear
dropped through me: that I wouldn't stay stuck together once
my parents were gone.

I hoped that wouldn't be true; that I was strong enough to
bend, not break.

  This is how we learn to stand alone, I think, we pull this love into
us and it sustains us. It remains. And it continues, even when we can
make more love of our own again. I hope that's how it works.

The world got bigger around me as I looked skywards. As it
had several years earlier when I stopped my hire car in Scotland
by a mountain near Fort William. But it wasn't a visual illusion; I
just felt myself expand into the growing space everywhere. I was
big and small at the same time and I didn't know how that was
so. At the dark heart of things, I found the sliver of comfort in
Nana's release.

For many nights, I'd welcome the forgetting that came with

sleep. Just before I succumbed, on that first night, I remembered: Nana had made me smile a few Christmases earlier when she'd said, "You want a man who's sorted himself out. They've usually done that by 40."

————

The next day Dave sent me a text:

 I'm here if you need me.

I called him from the car park of the supermarket, my car boot open and filled with bags of food I didn't want to eat.

"Hi. Thanks so much for your text," I said.

"Of course. Just wanted to let you know I'm here," he said.

"Thank you. I don't really know why I rang; I can't think of anything to say. I just needed..."

"That's okay. I know."

"That's the thing about death — what I can't get my head around — there's just *nothing* you can do."

"No, there isn't."

"They're just *not there* anymore. I mean, you think that's obvious, that's what death is. But I can't get past the nothingness of it."

"And you don't have to get past it. This will all have its own time."

Ten days later, I flew to London.

42

L ondon, you and me. Mostly, I walked you with purpose and ease: wholly present. Relief palpable. Your bridges — Lambeth, London and Waterloo — kept me high above the waters of the Thames as I criss-crossed the river, day and night.

My theatre cravings found new life at the Old Vic.

I wore a pair of Nana's earrings to Kew Gardens. Fine sterling silver hearts with tiny lengths of metal hanging from the bottom edges, their flayed ends like a peacock's tail. They tinkled in the breeze. She was with me, a gossamer. We sat in glorious late afternoon sunshine amid wispy grasses and bloom-laden branches — and springtime there made me feel like I could touch the very heartbeat of the Earth.

I bought a bright yellow notebook at the London Review Bookshop and wrote in it for the first time at Ruskin's Café.

Friends confided their plans, quiet fears and others' love stories, when we met in lounge rooms, libraries and bars.

But anxiety gnashed my body on the way to your City Airport, bound for the Channel Islands.

Not now.

Near the gate for my flight I got my shoes shined and when the man finished his handiwork, he said, "Just keep your sunglasses on when you board and you'll look like a rock star."

———

Mum and I met in Guernsey for a few days — the perfect pocket of seclusion, off the coast of France. We revelled in the sumptuousness of our new surrounds and unpacked ourselves into a shared space with a harbour view and a marble bathroom. Plush hotel aside, I knew not every mother and daughter could do that.

She'd been traversing the wilds of Scotland, again, and bubbled with a fresh brew of tales. Four international trips post-divorce and Mum's wanderlust was strong. I was grateful for all that meant; for her.

Rambling together on the tiny, car-free island of Sark, we found our rhythm. We rode with a young couple in the back of a horse-drawn cart and listened to a wry-humoured man recite the practised history of the place. It was fun but I was slightly distracted by the gargantuan diamond on the engagement ring of the woman opposite, her hands twirling in conversation but her body always touching her beau.

Another quick shot of luxury with Mum in Zurich, at the kind of hotel with room to land a helicopter.

"We could get used to this."

We split up for five days and would meet next in Singapore, to fly home.

Alone again, the familiar momentum of discovery pushed me out of Zürich Hauptbahnhof to Lucerne.

In search of gods and dragons and mystical things that give high places their allure, I stood at Mount Pilatus' peak. Shivering, I ate apple strudel in a cloud shroud at 2,132 metres

(6,995 feet). As I descended, the jester of a sun was re-
appearing.

I can hike down from halfway.

A jangled chorus of nearby cow bells made me smile. Little
yellow 'wanderweg' signs guided me past wildflowers in
meadows and postcard houses in forest clearings. But my quads
began to jelly. A little thread had been pulled in the back of my
mind. I tried to enjoy letting the world just wash around me.
Instead, everything began to slosh.

The next day's gloom magnified my distance from home.
The languages grated. I found the darker side of wandering:
when all the golden moments of discovery were forgotten. My
reference points slipped down the storm water drains with the
early morning rain. Outside seemed vaguely perilous. My
reflection in shop windows was as foreign to me as the streets
themselves.

Fondue will fix this!

When I found the restaurant, the heat and pungent sweet-
savoury fug in the tiny place pushed me back onto the street. In
the basement bathroom of a nearby old town café, tears sprang
quickly. I was adrift in the world instead of revelling. My heart
broke for Nana and Dad. I craved companionship. A fissure of
fear opened inside and catastrophes whirled within it.

One day later:

I wonder what's up there?

"Excuse me," I said to the group of students at the picnic
table while motioning towards the view, "I'm just going to take a
picture."

"Sure!"

Stepping off the hillside path into the small stone rotunda, I
smelled the beer and mused at their easy, laughing conversation
around the table. They didn't need to photograph Lucerne and
its lake aglow in twilight sun. It was just part of their slice of the

world; unremarkable. I nodded my thanks and continued further up the hill.

Then it stopped me. It filled me.

Singing. The group I had just left was a choir. Quietly, tentatively, they sought their harmonies with each other, voices spread across octaves. Finding their path within the piece and growing louder but somehow more delicate by the moment, their notes spilled into the evening air: a fusion of humanity and grace.

Their song drifted up the forested foothills, beguiling and transfixing. I dared not move. They were spinning magic into my soul. The sopranos deftly touched the high places I longed to reach; the basses, mellifluous, curled themselves into my neglected corners and made them hum.

The notes drifted and dispersed, little nothings in the twilight, never to be held but only felt as they became an elixir. I basked. As the sun slid further behind the hill, I watched the honeyed stone walls of the old town, looked up to the endless arc of sky and felt the kiss of night air on my hands.

I was being reassembled. I never knew the words but that serendipitous serenade lifted me beyond Lucerne and it said: 'Your song will come — even when you are adrift. Keep walking.'

43

Portland, Oregon. My first sight of you had been from the air. A patchwork of voracious greens, with a snail-trail silver-brown river: Willamette — rhymes with 'Janet', not 'Yvette'.

I bumped down through the dripping clouds.

On the ground, you were wet and cold to the touch. Drizzly. Too cold for summer.

An ice-slice wind tailed me as I walked your streets, ill-prepared for the temperature, until I fled into an outdoor apparel store and made the salesman happy with my command: "Make me warm again!"

You wielded your weirdness proudly — street art proclaiming it too — but we didn't gel. Not the first time. Two years earlier, spliced between San Francisco and Idaho, your oddities got under my skin: an invisible tattoo I didn't want.

There's no reason to come here again.

But there would be.

Now you're bright. I remember your city grid is a two-timer: to true and magnetic north. But I'm ignoring both and hoping that as long as I'm with you, this time, I'm heading in the right direction.

———

I tried to quicken my step but slow my heart. Striding through afternoon sunshine, not long off a flight from LA, I was trying to play it cool on my way to a downtown café. I was dressed too warmly — and it wasn't only the heat making me perspire.

It's just Dave. At the café. It's just a guy. You've been talking to him on the phone for 10 months. It's not like he's a stranger. It's not like this is a date; a blind date. No, it's not like that at all. There will be other people there. You're just friends. Perhaps? I don't know.

For once, Sara, just meet a guy and have a conversation. That's it. It's just talking — you know how to do that. You're friendly. It's okay. It's just a chat with some nice people.

It's just Dave.

It's actually pretty funny he's travelled from Sydney, you've come from Brisbane, and you're meeting for the first time in America!

Oh good. No pressure then.

I double-checked the address; my five-block walk from my hotel was done. My heart rate was sprint-fast.

It's so hot. Do I look sweaty? This is not how I planned it. Breathe.

I was at the café window; then at the door. There was nothing more to do.

Smile. Walk.

Don't smile like a crazy person.

"Hi! We finally meet!" I said to Marianne, who'd created the course where Dave and I 'met'. She smiled and we hugged hello.

"It's so good to see you! This is Karen — you already know Dave — and this is my partner," she said.

Smiles. Hugs. Handshakes.

I sat down and began immediately talking to Karen, on my left. She was a writer too, living in Edinburgh.

Dave was sitting directly opposite me.

Shit. He's cute. Be normal.

We played cat and mouse with glances across the circle.

I asked Marianne how her business was going and who else she knew at the World Domination Summit.

Eventually, I looked straight ahead, "So, Dave, here we are!"

He smiled. My brain went blank. We cobbled together the kind of conversation that happens when at least one person wants to make a good impression but wonders if everything has already been said on the phone.

I have no idea what he's thinking.

After about 45 minutes the group was disbanding. We all spilled back onto the street; it was festive. Everyone was gearing up for Fourth of July celebrations. The opening party for WDS was at the Portland Zoo that night.

"So, I'll see you at the party later?" Dave asked.

"Yeah. I'm just going to head back to the hotel for a while now, I'm a bit knackered," I said. I don't know if he remembered I'd only flown that day from LA, not Australia, but if so, he didn't say anything.

I phoned Dave at the zoo, while the party was in full swing. I was sitting on a wide internal window ledge in the corridor of my hotel, sun streaming upon me.

"I don't think I'm going to come tonight," I said.

"Okay, well if it's not something you feel like doing, don't force it," he replied.

I was used to hearing, "Come on! You'll enjoy it! It will be great fun! You'll love it once you're there." I was accustomed to that being my own monologue too. He said none of those things.

"Wow, may I just say what a lovely change it is to hear that sort of response," I said.

"Too many people spend too long doing things they don't want to just to please others. Do what *you* want."

"I actually just feel like getting a massage, takeaway from the food trucks and an early night. Then I'll be set for the weekend."

"Go for it. I'll give you a call later when we come back into town and see where you're at. If you don't answer, I'll know you're already asleep."

I was still awake at 11.30pm. Hovering between putting on pyjamas and whatever I had that would look good at the downtown bar Dave had invited me to. I paced between the wardrobe and bed; into the bathroom to look in the mirror again.

How tired do I look? Do I really want to go out now? We'll just have to be up again in a few hours... But it would be nice to go; hang out with some new people.

My pyjamas won.

Dave texted back and said he would meet me at my hotel in the morning and we'd go to the main WDS venue together.

————

Daytime spilled unevenly across a murky grey sky. Dave and I queued around the block for more than 30 minutes with about 2,800 others to enter the Newmark Theater — my stomach lurching with anticipation and anxiety the whole time; trying to keep my breakfast down and not worry that I didn't know where any bathrooms were.

We finally sat next to each other, just the two of us, as the lights went down for the first speaker at the event.

I felt the thrill I always did in a theatre. The room was a live thing; the atmosphere unlike any other I'd known. An energy danced through the crowd as entrepreneurs and business owners spoke sincerely and emphatically about making the most of life, about being brave and vulnerable and adventurous. About helping others.

I've found more of my people.

Mid-morning, as if we were teenagers who'd played truant and run off to the cinema, Dave put his hand on my thigh in the darkness. I put my hand on top of his and we interlaced fingers.

At morning break I was rife with emotion — elation, fear — and it knotted itself into a ball. It stripped me of the joy I craved. It catapulted through my brain and sat like lead in my throat as everyone was getting up to leave.

"I have to tell you something," I said to Dave as he was standing beside me, ready to join the exodus, but I was glued in place.

"What's that?"

"I...I have trouble with anxiety sometimes. And I don't know why but I'm feeling it right now." It was all I could manage.

His instant response: "What can I do? What do you need?"

"Um, I think I just need to sit here for a bit."

"Okay, do you want me to sit with you?"

"No, that's okay, you go."

"Well, how about I go and get you a glass of water? Would that help?"

"Yes, that would be good. Thank you."

We went to separate workshops in the afternoon and met back in the main theatre with everyone else early evening.

"Would you like to go for a drink?" Dave asked, after we kissed. Again.

"I live in Brisbane; you live in Sydney. I don't want to start something we don't finish. And I'm not after a weekend fling," I said.

"It's just a drink. We can figure anything else out later."

You're doing that whole thinking-too-far-ahead thing, Sara.

"Okay then. Sure. Yes."

Of course. Just a drink. I can do that.

We sat by the window at a small round dark timber table in my hotel bar and leaned towards each other as we talked. Even though we'd spoken on the phone for hours, it was marginally easier to understand Dave face to face. I'd known a guy from Newcastle on my first ship, but it was a thick accent at times.

We traded travel tales.

He always knew he'd leave home as soon as he could. After university, he'd rarely stayed in a job more than 18 months. Beyond the UK, he'd lived in California, Colorado and South Africa. Skydiving had been a favourite for years — his tally stood at about 240 jumps — and he grinned as he told me about rafting down the Zambezi.

When London had become a soul-crushing place, he'd moved to Australia nearly two years earlier and, in his spare time, became a triathlete.

"I'm never going to be the guy at the front of the race — but I'm not trying to be; I'm racing myself," he said. "Need to get back to training when I'm home though," he nodded to his beer glass as he tilted it. "All this, and the time off, is showing."

Hmmm. "I walk a lot," that's all I've got. *Though I did do fencing for a while...*

I already knew the bones of several of those stories but it was much more engaging to watch his expressions as he told them. To see the light shift in his blue eyes; to watch the same eyes wrinkle at the edges when a sly smile pulled up one corner of his mouth. To feel the boldness of his presence — its intensity — then feel everything shift and lighten when he chuckled.

———

The next morning, I paced, then felt woozy, then sat on the edge of my hotel bed. I was due to meet Dave downstairs in five minutes. A repeat of the previous day's plan. I couldn't do it. I texted him and told him I wasn't well. On the third text, at the time we were meant to meet, when he was clearly worried about me, I told the truth: anxiety was being a beast.

One of the worst bouts I'd had in many years had begun.

Why is this still happening to me?

Sweetheart, you've been through so much recently. It's okay. You're grieving. You're wondering what's going to happen with Dave; you're afraid all the shit that's rained down before might come again, just as you're happy. You don't want a long-distance relationship, not after what happened last time. You've borrowed money to come here and you're feeling like you owe it to your parents to have the best time, to justify their expense. But you owe it to yourself to just be. To have whatever time you need to have, without pressure, without expectation. Yes, you've come so far to be here but you're okay.

I hate feeling like this.

Remember that book you read, the 'it book', that showed you anxiety is a sign that things are out of balance, that you need to do things differently? Think differently?

Oh, yes.

Berating yourself for feeling this way doesn't help, does it?

*No, I remember now, I need to be kinder to myself. I **know** I can be confident, that I'm valuable; I'm just not **feeling** it right now.*

Not feeling it doesn't invalidate the truth of those statements. You've been knocked around a bit for the past while. We need a little 'fake it 'til you make it' here, I think. And you know, I'm not the only one who wants you to be okay. It seems there's a man out there waiting for you who wants you to be okay too. Don't shut him out. Trust this one. He seems like a good egg. Yes, I know the others did at first too, but this time might truly be different. Breathe. Deep breaths, that's it. Calm. Take another bite of apple; get something in your stomach. Go to the bathroom if you need to. That's what's great about nice hotel rooms: nice bathrooms! If

you're late to the conference today, that's okay. Take your time.
Breathe. It's all okay.

Maybe I could just stay here, order room service...

No. We're going to WDS. But let's break it down. Freshen up, grab
your handbag and let's just get to the other side of the door...That's it...
Now, down the hallway, into the lift...Keep going. Good...Out of the
hotel, across the road, along to the theatre...Yes, Dave's in there
somewhere, you don't have to see him now. Just find a seat...There you
go. Relax into it. You made it. Now, there's nothing for you to do; just
enjoy the speakers...A few deep breaths, that's it...You're doing well.
See, you made it.

Yes, I did. Okay, I can do this. I like the theatre. These are my
people. I want to be here. I'm glad I'm here.

Breathe.

The anxiety stayed, at high volume, most of the day. I sat on
my own in the theatre all morning. In the early afternoon, I
made cheery small-talk in the workshops that belied my inner
state.

A text from Dave mid-afternoon:

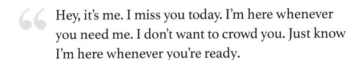

Hey, it's me. I miss you today. I'm here whenever
you need me. I don't want to crowd you. Just know
I'm here whenever you're ready.

The most rousing speeches of WDS came at the close of the
weekend. As a crowd, we cried; we stood and cheered. I thought
we were all broken open a little. We'd found a power in that
togetherness and it was achingly tender. I wanted to share it
with Dave; I wanted to hold his hand; I wanted him right there
with me. But I was an island amid it all, with more emotion than
I knew what to do with — anxiety, banished.

I rushed out the exit, just ahead of everyone else and went to
the side of the theatre I thought Dave would emerge from. His

face lit up when he saw me and I nearly bowled him over with the hug I wrapped him in.

"Are you okay?" he asked.

"I am now. Would you like to come to the closing party with me?" I asked.

"I'd love to."

We agreed to split up: change clothes, grab some food and — third time, lucky — Dave would meet me back at my hotel.

I could hear the first waves of music from Pioneer Square when I stepped out of the shower.

There are other people staying in hotels nearby who can hear this too — are they wondering what's going on?

I know! Soon I'll be there, in the thick of it. And it's going to be incredible.

Dave and I held hands as we walked to the Square.

"Let's call *this* our first date," I said, beaming.

He spotted faces in the crowd he knew from the previous year, and others he'd only met a few days before; we made rounds of introductions. I found a couple of people I'd been 'talking' to on Twitter and we laughed as we hugged and high-fived. Ironically, of course.

As the sun set to a Bollywood DJ, about 2,500 new friends rang in the night. I slipped into the music — it played through me: it pulsed in my chest and, on a neuro-chemical high, I could have kissed the sky.

I feel like phosphorescence.

Dave danced, by his own admission, like a geography teacher. But neither of us cared.

From the stage: "Let's hear it, Portland!"

"Wooohoooooo!"

Dance, dance. Dance like it's the last night of the world.

44

"So, when do you think you'll be able to come up?" I said into the phone a week later, a few hours after my flight from LA had landed, and Brisbane lay beyond my window again.

"Well, now I've checked the calendar," Dave said, "with training and competitions it won't be for another three weeks, unfortunately."

"Three weeks? That's too long. I'm coming down."

I had to reduce the space between us.

A few days later, holding my red carry-on suitcase — the Sydney Harbour Bridge and Opera House flanking my view at Circular Quay — I looked across the water to the shore-hugging buildings at Kirribilli while I waited for the ferry.

I'll be at Dave's in about an hour.

He had left his key for me to pick up while he was at work, and it was waiting as described.

As I stepped out of the lift into an interior hallway, for a moment, I felt like I was on a hotel-reviewing trip: the carpet soft underfoot, lighting muted within a neutral colour scheme. I scanned for the correct apartment number, a squirrelling anticipation in my stomach, even though he wasn't going to be home for another hour or two.

In one of our phone conversations months earlier, we'd agreed it would be lovely to live in a place painted white, with floor-to-ceiling windows. I saw why he so readily thought that was a good idea. I abandoned my handbag and suitcase by the kitchen bench and my body softened into the couch. All I could smell was washing powder, or something fresh. The room: spacious, clean, sparsely-furnished — racing bike sitting in the corner.

There's no complete memory for the next four days and five nights, just vignettes.

I was on my own, then a key scratched in the lock and Dave appeared, his white business shirt dropped him into an image I'd never had of him but he looked smart; his embrace as strong as my delight; slightly uncoordinated kisses that made me feel like a teenager.

We'll get the hang of that again.

"It's so good to see you," he said.

This is crazy.

We each set up our laptops on the dining table and attended to our own screens for a while.

"I can't usually work with anyone else around," I said. Usually, neither could he.

Dave cooked dinner. We sat opposite each other and talked; it was so easy. Other nights: we conjured life wish lists while we ate takeaway, bundled together under the quilt on the sofa bed that we'd made up in the lounge room so we could watch big-screen movies in decadent comfort.

We walked by the water, an inlet from the Parramatta River.

"I can't believe you live on Kendall Bay," I said, "I was actually born in Sydney but grew up near a tiny town called Kendall. No one has ever heard of it — unless they've caught the

XPT north from here, then sometimes people vaguely recognise the name because the only big thing Kendall had left was a railway station. And even that had a half-size platform."

"It's near Port Macquarie, isn't it?"

"How do you even know that?"

"I've raced in Port," he grinned.

I asked him every question I could think of — an exhaustive list built upon what I already knew of his past, and his dreams. I dug for all his skeletons; I unearthed a few more of mine. We compared corpses. He bore my sporadic inquisition with grace.

On the Saturday night, I donned a red dress and heels and accompanied Dave to his triathlon club presentation dinner, repressing anxiety and perspiring the whole way there in the car but determined to have a wonderful time. I giggled at something he said as I was taking my stockings off again when we got home and just as Dave turned toward me in the bedroom doorway, laughing, I took a photo on my phone — it was a little blurry but I could still see his eyes shining with pure impish glee.

———

Good old Brissie afternoon showers.

The air became thick and rumbling and the restless legs feeling kicked in, and I walked out into the first *drop, drop, drop* anyway. I needed the streets, the houses, the cinema, the oval — all the familiar things around me — as I moved.

Hawthorne streets. 'My' streets.

Think of all the times you've walked past these beautiful Queenslanders, so exquisitely renovated.

I still wonder if the people who own them have time to really live in them.

My strides were longer, as if the rain had restored me; my back licked with perspiration.

Do you want to look back and know you didn't do this because you were afraid?

There is so much of me that is not though. This is not like before.

My body tingled. My mind danced.

Jacarandas would be flowering again soon, their sumptuous purple-blossomed beauty flashing against the sky across swathes of the city, then carpeting the ground.

I stretched my calves while leaning against a bollard at the park and replayed my favourite conversation from Dave's two-day visit. I'd been leaning against my kitchen bench:

"If you need me, if you *really* need me, just call. I will close my computer, I will leave the office, I will drive to the airport and I will get on a plane," he'd said.

"You'd *truly* do that?"

He looked me in the eye. Unwavering.

"Yes."

I knew he'd move to Brisbane if I asked.

———

"What if it doesn't work out?" The Counsellor asked.

"I'll start over. Again. We know how much practice I've had at that," I said.

"Worst case scenario?"

"I'll come back, find another job. And see what I see."

"I'm so, so happy for you, Sara."

"I couldn't have done it without you. Thank you."

"No — you've done all the work."

"Um, would it be appropriate to give you a hug? I've known you for so long and…"

She laughed and stepped towards me with open arms, "Sure, we can do that today."

Thank you. Thank you.

I cradled my peppermint tea in both hands as Mum and I talked on her patio; I was trying to drink everything in.

"I'm surprised you're still here," she said.

"Yeah, me too. I've been in Brisbane since 2005," I said.

"*Eight years.* Thought you'd have gone long ago!" she smiled.

"I guess it's taken this long to find the right place *to* go."

My phone rang.

"Oh, sorry, it's Dave."

"You answer that." Mum scooped up her empty coffee cup and took it back to the kitchen.

Forty-five minutes disappeared as I chatted, relishing the sun; I hung up and went back inside.

"Where you at, Ma?" I called.

Her muffled reply came from the direction of the garage. I'd squeezed my car next to hers the evening before last, the whole interior except for the driver's seat a ramshackle mess of my belongings that weren't going on the truck, shoved in as I'd raced against the night to get my apartment cleaned and emptied.

Mum was just pulling a blanket across the top of my newly arranged, ordered, nested, stacked, protected cargo.

"Oh, Ma, you just did all this now? You're amazing. Thank you!"

"Well, you know I would have come to help you pack," she said, "but at least I could help you with what's here now."

"Don't worry about it at all. You have moved my stuff every other time we've gone anywhere and it's only now that I can *truly* appreciate that — it just took four weeks to get to this point; I obviously still have too much! You've been a lifesaver. Is your hip okay?"

"It's fine," she waved the question away. By her own

assertion, she didn't 'do' ageing, and we both thought that was wonderful.

The following morning, Mum waved me goodbye from the edge of her driveway and started to cry. But she was trying so hard not to. I kept my Cheshire Cat grin as wide as I could. Tucked away, I still had a little red bag with orange lining. I stuck my hand out the window, waved, then tapped a friendly *honk-honk*. A see-you-soon honk. Not a goodbye honk. She was coming to visit the following month, "once you're a bit settled".

It was so hard to turn the first few corners — the pulling away was palpable, as it had never been before. I wanted to cry too but I had to think about who and what I was going *towards*. I could hear Mum's voice: "Dad and I raised you to be independent. Don't ever think you should stay in one place because of me. The world's your oyster, girl!"

————

In early September, five weeks and a 1,000-kilometre (600 mile) drive after my stay at Dave's, I let myself into his apartment again. It was 2pm. He was at work. A removal truck with the remainder of my belongings was due to arrive in three days.

I was 35. It was 2013.

There was a colourful bunch of fresh flowers on the dining table and a card that read:

 Welcome home, sweetheart.

EPILOGUE

I was almost 38. It was February 2016. Time expanded in the twilight — in the Southern Highlands of New South Wales — amid the folds of tree-framed paddocks and hills, under a cloud-cut sky. A final sun streak illuminated the strappy agapanthus leaves outside the cottage kitchen window. The lawn glowed and the old highway that ribboned past was bright-slick from an earlier shower.

I remember how this push into darkness in the country draws out the quiet, too.

Birds had settled early; there were no crickets rustling yet. The wiry hum of the fridge was the only sound in the wooden house. There was no internet there: experience was rendered glimmering poplar leaves and damp earth and the act of switching on a lamp by the fireplace, as the evening curled into valleys and onto the sharp air that slipped under the front door.

All cities are another time.

Dave was at breakfast in the other hemisphere. Work encroached into his meals there too; we'd just spoken briefly.

In my precious, tended solitude there in the Highlands, I had begun to write — and delete and rewrite — the fragile lines

that split and whorled themselves into paragraphs: the first
pages of my book.

I know what happens, but I've no idea where this will take me.

Early, early morning sunlight tumbled through the cottage
and me, beckoning. I pushed into the verdant garden and
wondered at the spiderwebs laced with dew-drop pearls,
gleaming — so exquisite in the rust-gold of a new day.

———

One February day in New York City I turned 39. It was 2017.

That was two days ago.

I'm waiting at a pedestrian crossing in Manhattan, at W22nd
St and 7th Ave, it's the edge of the day and the sun is chasing
shadows elsewhere, beyond the island, and it feels like I could
run into a hep-cat kinda place, straight outta Beat world, with its
jazz and poets and black-ripple midnights, where I could drink
in the elsewhereness of each step.

And in this moment, I'm too warm in my new jacket, not
quite believing a snow storm is due in a few hours.

*Will waking up in a whitened New York feel like the first time I
saw snow falling in London, all those aeons ago?*

The 'Walk' sign pushes me and the sidewalk stragglers into
motion again and I'm exhaling as I stride across the thick white
lines, gloveless hands out of my pockets and enjoying their
freedom.

*There is something in this moment, here in Chelsea; I just don't
know what. All I can think is 'Run, run into the liquid night...'*

I'll tell Dave about this sensation when we're both home in
Sydney again. Home — in a way I've never known — its
topography and climate charted between the two of us. A
crucible that is sanctuary and smelter.

I'll tell him when he's back from London and we've almost

thrown off our jet lag. When we're trading tales and making plans at dinnertime, the dining table bright with one of Nana's tablecloths and stacked travel books.

But I already know what he'll say about this feeling.

"Yes, sometimes you just have to listen to that."

I'm walking 7th Ave. Lower Manhattan is much further ahead.

Maybe I'll look out across the water there before I go.

Either way, it doesn't matter. I'll always go. My life bends to the habit and I am richer for it.

Enjoy this? There's more.

VIP access to the GO bonus extras (only available here):
www.hellosaramoss.com/vip

ACKNOWLEDGMENTS

I read somewhere it takes a village to raise a book. There are so many people who've been directly or indirectly instrumental in shaping what you've just read, and I'd like to extend my heartfelt thanks to them all.

Specifically:

Alain de Botton — for your tireless production of a deft body of work that articulates and illuminates so much of what it is to be human. *The Art of Travel* gave me the first truest understanding that I wasn't alone.

Tom Hodgkinson — for *How to be Idle*, which gave me an inkling of how to actually relax; and for your work with The School of Life team in creating an unforgettable weekend in North Devon, UK.

Claire Bidwell Smith — for replying when I wrote in 2007 to tell you how much I enjoyed your writing; for continuing to bring the hardest, darkest parts of life to the light so others may heal through their grief. For your gentle but adroit advice, editing and friendship.

Barbara Sher — your wisdom, humour and practical take

on making the most of a personality that thrives on curiosity has been nothing short of life changing. In a good way.

Marianne Cantwell — for your verve. For being my introduction, in more ways than one, to another life.

Tara Gentile — for your speech near Oregon's Mt Hood, to an eager gathering of fledgling entrepreneurs, at Chris Guillebeau's Pioneer Nation in October 2015. During your keynote, I saw my freelance editing business as the most elaborate and lovingly-constructed organism for procrastination. In that moment, I knew one thing to be true above all: it was time to write my book.

Mark McGuinness — for empathetically writing a suite of books all creatives should have in their arsenal.

Peter Shallard — for creating a psychologically comprehensive goal-setting process. Headstart 2016 was a fundamental part of my preparation and planning for writing GO. A shout out to 'Coach Alex' too, for keeping me on track in the beginning, and for so much more prior to that.

Shawn Coyne and Tim Grahl — for melding wit, courage and experience to bring the Story Grid universe to life; for empowering writers by sharing deeply practical ways to understand and craft effective stories. I was in the wilderness before I found you.

Willo Sana — for the beautiful way you show up in the world. For reflecting your faith in me to take this story to the dark places it needed to go, so the light ones would mean so much more.

My beta team extraordinaire — Dixe, El, James, Sara, Kathy, Vicky, Beck, Margaret, Alex, Lauren, Daniel and Stacey, for your thoroughness, generosity and candour. This couldn't be what it is without you. Hat tip to Daniel for also being my unwavering 'check in buddy' and milestone celebrator during the first draft. Extra kudos to El, who was there for the long haul.

Emily O'Neill and Alissa Dinallo — Emily, for your patience, humility and introduction to Alissa; Alissa, for your willing collaboration and masterful cover creation.

Megan Hills — for your incisive mind, kind heart, and blurb wizardry. For keeping pom-poms at the ready for so many years.

Dan Gilmore — for your insightful and thoughtful encouragement throughout this project and beyond.

Jane Walters — for listening. Ad nauseam. And still cheering. And still showing up for tea. You're a gem.

Amanda Doughty, Kenny Campbell, Jenn Pelley and Kate Haggman — for your steadfast friendship during the past decade (or two), across oceans, time zones and name changes.

The Sydney Live Your Legend crew; The Great Escape Artists; WDSers and PN2015 folks — your heart and hard-earned knowledge brought to life- and business-wrangling have been a source of joy and camaraderie for several years.

Dave — for belief that these pages (sight unseen for years) were worth creating, and your efforts in making them so. I am boundlessly grateful for your faith in me.

Cherie and Grant — my parents, for all you give and who you are. For honouring yourselves during your 10 years apart, and for doing the same when you remarried. I'm so glad you found your way back to each other.

Finally, if you've found yourself within this story — thank you for being part of my life.

ABOUT THE AUTHOR

Sara Moss is an Australian writer, explorer (of places and ideas), design lover and occasional photographer. She's worked with big and small business, entrepreneurs, governments, travel guides and magazines — mostly as a writer; also as a researcher, editor, photographer and, for a little while, a UX and CX practitioner.

Now Sara lives on Sydney's Northern Beaches with her partner. She blends solitude and collaboration to make beautiful books.

www.hellosaramoss.com

instagram.com/hellosaramoss

facebook.com/hellosaramoss

twitter.com/hellosaramoss

Lightning Source UK Ltd.
Milton Keynes UK
UKHW040831170919
349933UK00001B/42/P

9 780648 260523